THE SECRETS TO
OUTLINING YOUR NOVEL

HOW TO CLEARLY ORGANIZE YOUR STORY IDEAS INTO AN EPIC BOOK YOU CAN WRITE AND PUBLISH

JOHN S WARNER

THE SECRETS TO OUTLINING YOUR NOVEL

HOW TO CLEARLY ORGANIZE YOUR STORY IDEAS INTO AN EPIC BOOK YOU CAN WRITE AND PUBLISH

JOHN S. WARNER

© **Copyright John S Warner 2022 - All rights reserved.**

The content contained within this book may not be reproduced, duplicated or transmitted without direct written permission from the author or the publisher.

Under no circumstances will any blame or legal responsibility be held against the publisher, or author, for any damages, reparation, or monetary loss due to the information contained within this book. Either directly or indirectly. You are responsible for your own choices, actions, and results.

Legal Notice:

This book is copyright protected. This book is only for personal use. You cannot amend, distribute, sell, use, quote or paraphrase any part, or the content within this book, without the consent of the author or publisher.

Disclaimer Notice:

Please note the information contained within this document is for educational and entertainment purposes only. All effort has been executed to present accurate, up to date, and reliable, complete information. No warranties of any kind are declared or implied. Readers acknowledge that the author is not engaging in the rendering of legal, financial, medical or professional advice. The content within this book has been derived from various sources. Please consult a licensed professional before attempting any techniques outlined in this book.

By reading this document, the reader agrees that under no circumstances is the author responsible for any losses, direct or indirect, which are incurred as a result of the use of the information contained within this document, including, but not limited to, — errors, omissions, or inaccuracies.

CONTENTS

Introduction — 11

1. A CLEAN SLATE— THE BASICS OF OUTLINING — 19
   What is a Novel Outline? — 20
   Why Novel Outlines Work in Your Favor — 22
   Understanding What Type of Writer You Are on the Plotter to Panster Scale — 29

2. DIFFERENT TYPES OF OUTLINES TO CHOOSE FROM — 33
   The Snowflake Method — 35
   The Agenda Method — 38
   The Bookend Method — 39
   The Beat Method — 39
   The Three Acts Method — 41
   The Tree Method — 42
   The Synopsis Method — 43
   The In-depth Method — 43
   The Bulleted Method — 44
   The Excel Method — 45
   The Visual Method — 46
   The John S. Warner Method — 47

3. DEVELOPING A PLOT AND FILLING PLOT HOLES WITH WHAT IFS — 51
   Building an Outline with What Ifs — 57
   How to Fill Those Annoying Plot Holes — 59
   Should Subplots Be Outlined? — 60

4. MAKING SENSE OF THE SETTING AND TIMELINE — 63
   Understanding the Setting and Timeline — 64
   Creating a Vivid Setting — 67

How to Organize your Timeline 70
How Michael Crichton Created a Timeline
with Plot Cards 72

5. **GROWING CHARACTERS THAT CAPTIVATE THE READERS** 75
   What does a Writer Need to Know About
   Their Characters? 76
   30 Questions to Create a Character Outline 78
   How Should Characters Develop Throughout
   the Timeline? 81
   Character Outline Template 86

6. **BREAKING DOWN THE BRILLIANCE INTO CHAPTERS** 89
   What Should Each Chapter Contain 90
   How to End a Chapter 93
   Should Chapters be Named? 95
   Is There an Ideal Length for a Chapter? 95

7. **OUTLINE ADVICE FOR CHILDREN'S BOOKS** 99
   Extra Considerations for a Children's Book
   Outline 100
   How does Julia Donaldson Outline her Books? 102
   Roald Dahl's Writing Technique 103
   The Incredible Mind of Dr. Seuss 104
   Points to Remember 105

8. **OUTLINE ADVICE FOR ROMANCE NOVELS** 111
   What Does a Romance Novel Need? 112
   What Can We Take from the Author of The
   Notebook 119
   Simplicity and Complexity of Jane Austen 121

9. **OUTLINE FOR THRILLER AND HORROR NOVELS** 125
   Be Specific About the Subgenre 126
   5 Elements to Include in Your Thriller/Horror
   Outline 127

H.P. Lovecraft and His Handwritten Horror	129
The Story of Dean Koontz	130
Words of a Bestseller Teacher	132
10. OUTLINE ADVICE FOR WAR AND HISTORY NOVELS	135
How to Prepare Your Historical Fiction	136
William Faulkner's *A Fable* Outline	140
Editing a Children's War Story	141
The Pillars of Ken Follett's Outlines	142
11. OUTLINE ADVICE FOR CRIME AND DETECTIVE NOVELS	143
Templates for your Crime Novels	144
More than an Inspiration for Novel Outlining	147
How an Arctic Trip was the Muse Behind Sherlock Holmes	148
The Queen of Irish Crime Fiction	149
12. OUTLINE ADVICE FOR POPULAR FICTION	153
What Makes a Novel that Appeals to the Many	154
What Does a Popular Fiction Novel Need?	156
Jodi Picoult and Her Structure	157
Outline Conclusion	161
More from John S Warner	169
Bibliography	171

THE SECRETS TO OUTLINING YOUR NOVEL

How to clearly organize your story ideas into an epic book you can write and publish

By John S. Warner

FREE GIFT

Just for You!
A FREE GIFT TO OUR READERS

Please enjoy this 20-page workbook to create the best positive Character arc for your protagonist. Easy to follow Step by Step Guide

Scan the QR code below.

Or go to https://johnswarner.activehosted.com/f/1.

INTRODUCTION

> *"I don't start a novel until I have lived with the story for a while to the point of actually writing an outline. And after a number of books, I've learned that the more time I spend on an outline, the easier the book is to write. And if I cheat on the outline, I get in trouble with the book"*
>
> — JOHN GRISHAM

Writing is a lonely profession, with its unique highs and lows, moments of inspiration, and complete writer's block, which no one but the writer can truly understand. When I started my journey into the world of writing three decades ago, I had only one plan – to write the book of my dreams, to write my masterpiece. Like every average Joe rookie writer, I started with a bagful of fresh ideas, a babble of voices from my characters, conflicting tracks, and multiple plotlines, but no structural principle to back it up with.

On some days, I would wake up in the wee hours of the night, feel inspired and scribble. Sometimes I would come home from the coffee shop with my pockets stuffed with paper napkins, crammed with impromptu writing notes. And then, there were days when not a single syllable popped out of the pen. Days rolled into weeks, and not one substantial sentence came out of my head. So then, I took a deliberate break from writing, sat myself down, and read more about the craft of writing.

From E.M. Forster's *Aspects of the Novel* to Stephen King's *On Writing: A Memoir of the Craft*, my readings made me understand that what I was lacking was neither creativity nor language skills, neither fresh ideas nor imagination, but a plan, a proper blueprint for the book. That explained the extended writer's block; I was simply lost in the wondrous woods of creativity without a map.

There are several reasons new writers suffer from writer's block and give up. Your mind can be pregnant with umpteen good ideas competing to pour forth onto the paper, but you aren't confident enough to write as you might be feeling you lack the knowledge or the tools required to write. You have ideas but do not know how to structure these ideas. Hence it's always an unconcluded piece. Sometimes, even if you finish your writing, you are taken over by self-doubt – is it good enough, will people read it? In those moments, a well-planned book outline can act as the conscience-keeper of the directionless artist in you. It keeps you from second-guessing your creative choices and, while writing, makes you more confident in the craft as now you have a plan.

However, easier said than done, and a well-drawn-out book outline can take months and months to finish. It can be challenging as you must know what to include and be doubly sure what to exclude to make your novel a well-knit, well-structured piece of writing. So, is there a science to the art of curating complete and well-organized book outlines? Is there a step-by step formula to design your novel's journey before penning it down? Yes, there is.

This book is the outcome of my experiments and experiences devising compact and organic book outlines, a journey that has taken many years. It will take you through the outlining processes, which involve visualizing the destination and then charting out the most exciting way for your characters to reach it, based on causality, probability, and logical, cause-effect relations between incidents in the novel. It's practically like envisioning the last sentence before writing the first. As Joyce Carol Oates puts it, "The first sentence can't be written until the final sentence is written."

The practice of creating book outlines has helped almost every writer in their career, including stalwarts like Mark Twain. According to Twain, "The secret of getting ahead is getting started. The secret to getting started is breaking your complex overwhelming tasks into small manageable tasks and then starting on the first one. Creating an outline for your book helps with that."

The outline doesn't have to be perfect, and the idea is to make sure every scene leads into another one, keeping the flow of your story on track. It doesn't have to be fancy either; a simple list will do. You can find loose ends and incoherence in your plot and make corrections much more efficiently during the outlining phase.

A well-drawn outline helps keep an intricate and character-heavy storyline clear to the readers. Let's try to understand this with an example. We are all familiar with *Harry Potter*, whether in the book or the movie version. J.K. Rowling wrote the books in seven parts on which the eight films were based. Each book has various characters, multiple wizarding families and clans, interrelated motives and plotlines, and a coming-of-age timeline for the main characters. Do you believe that the world-renowned J.K. Rowling, whom twelve publishers rejected before the first *Harry Potter* book saw the light of the day, could have done it without a clearly drawn-out book plan? Wouldn't she be lost in the maze of characters and motives of her creation if there wasn't a seven-book plan ready, even before the publication of *Harry Potter and the Philosopher's Stone*?

In an Endpaper blog, we get a sneak peek into Rowling's mind; when she showed how she mapped chapters 13-24 of the fifth *Harry Potter* book. It was jotted down on paper, neatly divided into columns representing chapter numbers, timeline, and plot points to track the development. By creating a clear-cut book outline, one can write even a mammoth project like the seven books of *Harry Potter*.

So what's stopping you from taking the next step toward creating a well-defined outline? This book will equip you with the tools to create a logical and organic system for your novels. By the end of this book, you will be able to answer these questions for yourself:

1. What is a book outline, and what isn't?
2. How does an overview give you a clear picture of your project's pros and cons and dos and don'ts?
3. How does an outline save time by offering your book a well-defined direction?
4. How to beat writer's block and self-doubt by finalizing your book outline?
5. What are the different methods of putting together a blueprint for your book?
6. How to convert a vague idea into a concrete book outline?
7. What are the plot elements, and what are the strategies to bridge the gaping holes in your plotline?
8. How to create a proper setting for your story?
9. How to track the timeline and map the characters' actions to the timeline?
10. How to build and develop a character that draws in the readers?

11. How do you design a chapter-wise break up for your book while organically maintaining the flow and transition?
12. How to contrive a perfect end to the chapters?

Once you are comfortable answering these questions, you are on the right track to chalking out an outline for your novel. This book will add the theories of successful book outlines and give you a taste of the inner workings of a blueprint by discussing how book outlines are created for different writing genres – from children's literature and romance to thrillers.

Outlining your novel can seem like a lot of work, but it's worth it. Trust me; you'll be glad you did it! Besides the practical aspect, a book outline is evidence of your creative journey and birth as a writer. Not every novel will become a one-shot success like Emily Bronte's classic *Wuthering Heights* or Jo Rowling's magical *Harry Potter* series, but every book written is an opportunity to improve with the next one. An outline allows you to look back at your theory and reckon what worked and what didn't. It gives you a reality check on re-strategizing your creative approach.

There are several ways of writing a novel, but not every way will suit everyone. You need to find the one that works best for you and outlining gives you a panoramic view of that creative path. With every book's outline, I have learned what works and what doesn't and finally reached a point where I can share the accumulated wisdom of all these years with those aspiring but struggling to take the first step in novel writing. This approach has worked like magic for me, and I hope it does the same for you.

So without further ado, let's start building a roadmap to the book of your dreams!

1

A CLEAN SLATE— THE BASICS OF OUTLINING

I can remember my earliest lessons in classical literature and still recall when the professor introduced Aristotle's *Poetics* to explain the importance of a well-knit plot. If a similar experience doesn't haunt you, let me briefly explain. Aristotle's theory of tragedy hinges on the significance of a plot with a proper beginning, middle, and end. This theory is the only acceptable way to satisfy a reader. What have you got without any of those three?

If I can rewind a few more years – elementary school, essay writing class, what did my teacher say about writing a good essay? First, it must have a proper beginning or introduction, a body or middle where you develop the central idea, and a conclusion that draws all your ideas together and gives the final takeaway. However, having a beginning, a middle, and an end only paints a picture with broad brush strokes. A proper outline for your book provides a more intricate and organized approach to arranging that beginning, middle, and end in a chaptered plotline. From my earliest lessons in writing to my earliest lessons in literary studies and creative writing, I was continuously trained to develop a sense of structure and a coherence of form.

Let's look into what an outline is and what it is not.

WHAT IS A NOVEL OUTLINE?

A novel outline comes in many forms, but it is a prioritized list of events in your story. And if it were a basic list, the essential things would be at the top, and the least critical items will be at the bottom.

Outlining your novel before writing gives your writing process a proper direction without interfering with your creative process. Instead, it streamlines your creative process as an outline can be incremental and flexible, allowing innovative changes when needed.

An outline is called many names by different people. Some call it a skeleton, some a roadmap or a blueprint for your novel. Whatever terminology you find apt, the book outline is a document that includes plot, character, settings, scenes, timelines, events, incidents, and logical connections to give your storyline a structure.

By outlining your novel, you can see the bigger picture – exactly where each scene fits into the story, where each character is headed, and how the different parts are connected. A novel outline answers three most important questions any writer can ask:

1. What is the main takeaway from the story? This question makes you think with clarity on author commitment – does your book resolve all the promises you made to your reader?
2. What timeline, pressures, and challenges are working on your characters?
3. What are the stakes and conflicts? For what reason is the protagonist fighting? Are the characters' plotline pressures developing as the narrative proceeds?

Once you find answers to these pressing concerns, the rest of the writing journey becomes a cakewalk.

So what should a novel outline look like? Do we have a set format or protocol for outlining? Does every author create a strategy? Let's begin by answering the last question. No, every writer has a different creative journey and different creative tools in their kitty. Some believe in starting with a proper blueprint, and some go with their creative flow and instincts. In the literary world, the writers who prefer working with an outline are called 'plotters,' and the best-known 'plotters' are Ernest Hemingway, Mark Twain, John Grisham, and J. K. Rowling.

There's no straightforward answer to the other two questions about the outline format! You can write a one-pager skeleton or a comprehensive document with detailed diagrams and flowcharts for visualization, or you can have flashcards attached to a clipboard like a concrete storyboard. We shall discuss the different methods of outlining in the next chapter.

No one can say how long or short an ideal book outline should be. It depends on your storyline's complexity, genre, and length.

However, you must not confuse an outline with your first draft. An outline is the gist or summary of your entire work. For instance, you have a plan of ten chapters and write two lines for each in a word doc, which makes an outline. But when you expand each chapter to the full length and finish writing the entire book, that's your first draft, a rough version of your complete book. But that's a discussion for another book. As of now, let's focus on how outlines can help your writing process.

WHY NOVEL OUTLINES WORK IN YOUR FAVOR

Writing is a highly subjective process, and no two great writers can ever agree on the best way to proceed. So even whether or not to start with an outline, the literary world is divided. Therefore, before deciding in favor of outlining, you must sensitize yourself to all the pros and cons involved in the process because what works for me may or may not work for you when it comes to creative writing.

Before peering into the pros, let's note the cons. There are popular misconceptions or myths about outlining a book. Some writers believe that outlining is extra work, a sheer waste of time. Why not let the story take its course and take a creative life of its own? Some believe that an outline can be an imposition; it can restrict creativity. Though it's your outline, and you are at creative liberty to pull and stretch at whichever point you want, having a strategy can often limit your creative flight as you may try to be too committed to it. Excellent writing often flourishes in those moments of epiphany, those 'eureka' moments when an ingenious solution to a plot complexity makes its way to you. You already have reverse engineered a solution to the conflict by having an outline.

There's also a chance that strict adherence to an outline can lead to a shorter piece of writing as you only invest in expanding your book's synopsis. Another theory looks at outlining as an extra step taken for nothing. The first drafts are always a work in progress. A book takes shape only after rounds of revision, beta reading, and incremental and developmental edits. Investing too much time in the outline is like investing too much effort in the skeleton of the first draft, which will not be the final product.

I do not disregard the opinions of fellow artists, but I also cannot encourage you to think of these as gospel truth.

When discussing the benefits of having a book outline as the first step to writing your novel, the reason will be crystal clear.

Here are some advantages of having an outline ready before you write:

It gives your creativity a better direction.

A good outline gives your story a proper direction and makes writing easier. It's like finding your way to an unknown country with a compass and a map. The outline helps you see the bigger picture, a panoramic view of the story to see how everything fits together. Take the example of a jigsaw puzzle board. The border of the board tells you which pieces go into the four corners, then one after the other, you assemble the right fitting piece and finish the frame. An outline does just that for your story; it gives you an overarching structure for all of your novel's major scenes, events, characters, situations, and plot points and ensures the flow is logical.

It minimizes the chance of writers' block.

When you have an outline, you have a blueprint for the following

- How your significant characters think
- What timeline maps their actions?

- What are the major complexities and possible resolutions from the perspective of your major characters?
- A rough estimate of how many chapters will be and what leads to what

It becomes easier to sit yourself down and write when you have a plan. Unfortunately, creative people often suffer from droughts or dry spells (the dreaded writer's block). If you struggle with writing and have no clear idea or plan of where your book is headed, these dry spells can stretch longer than usual. An outline will not eliminate those creative dry spells but will give you a direction to think and try to recover.

Having an outline ready to go will make it easier to get back into writing your story. When you have a clear picture of what is going on in the story and want to add more detail to your outline, writer's block can be swatted away much more quickly. Thus, having a procedure brings you one step closer to having a plan for finishing the book.

Finding plot holes becomes much more accessible.

A book-length project can continuously develop several continuity issues or loose ends in the plot. An outline helps you keep tabs on the major plot points and significant developments. Still, the minor and minute details grow out of these critical developments, and any situation can turn into a plot hole. For instance, some character traits define your protagonist's journey. Those big picture qualities should always remain intact, but minor details often break the spell for the reader. For example, early in a story, I mentioned that the protagonist couldn't swim, and then later in the story, he dove into a river to chase after the antagonist. This kind of mistake can be disturbing and indigestible to the reader if you don't pick up on it. More problematic are the timeline issues, especially if you use flashbacks. You may show the character had lost her father in an accident twenty years ago and then later in the story forget and explain an incident from ten years ago with the same dead father. This mistake can be a major plot hole, but it's easy to do without a proper plan, especially with complicated stories. Outlines done correctly will make these mistakes glaringly obvious, but someone writing by the seat of their pants may not notice.

An outline keeps all these continuity issues under control for seamless reading. For example, if a character is doing something that doesn't make sense, is not true to their type of person, or is not mapping to the timeline, it will be much easier to spot when written down in your outline and fix the problem before you write your book.

Easier character development

There are two types of characters: round and flat. On the one hand, you have rounded characters that develop or become different people throughout their journey in the novel; they follow an arc. I wrote about this in great detail in "The Secrets to Creating Character Arcs," but basically, it means your character changes along the journey, sometimes for the bad and sometimes not, depending on your story. On the other hand, getting back to this story, flat characters remain the same from beginning to end. Round characters are always considered more exciting and intriguing in literature. No matter how your character is portrayed, as round or flat, they need to have a journey, and the book outline helps you carve the course each of your significant characters will take.

The characters' mind and development, good, bad, or in the morally gray area, is shaped by their response to the experiences and events they go through in their life throughout the novel's plot. By etching an outline, you give your characters a more realistic path to grow and develop or remain flat if they choose to. Their responses and reactions to situations, conflicts, complexities, and other characters remain highly plausible if an outline guides them, and you will see this development easily in an overview. Concentrating on the plot in your strategy makes it easier to see how your character would react, so you change them according to the situation.

The actual writing becomes more straightforward.

When you plan to write a book, you know what you want to accomplish before you write it. Your characters are already well defined from the outline to write the story quickly. This tactic means that your entire manuscript will be easier to write and flow better because it makes better sense. Don't get me wrong, writing a novel is not easy, but doing the heavy lifting at the start means that the end process is more straightforward.

The average novel consists of about 200-250 pages and can be written in about 3-4 months. You are probably a good writer if you can write a novel of this size without breaking the tempo. I have worked with many people who should have been able to write the first draft much faster than they did because they simply didn't have the enthusiasm and motivation required to keep pushing through and finishing the book. There is a straightforward formula to "keep at it" – writing every day. A well-knit outline helps to keep at it and complete your writing on the scheduled time. And having an outline ensures that you have a plan; you have something to write daily.

Many new writers often get the purpose of doing an outline before a first draft all mixed up. Let me remind you that the two are different. Let's try to understand the difference with a metaphor of bread baking. You gather the flour, yeast, salt, and oil and make the dough. It won't be perfect when you bake the first loaf of bread. Only through several attempts will you bake the perfect loaf. The first draft is the first loaf of bread, and the outline is the list of ingredients and the recipe.

A first draft throws the ingredients together and then looks for mistakes and improvements. An outline knows the ingredients you need, planning the process and leaving room for extra elements along the way. There should be enough detail for direction but not so rigid there isn't room to explore plots and characters. Now, if I ask you if having an outline will make writing the first draft easier or not, what will your answer be?

But, yet again, I would urge you to hold that thought and answer after you know what type of a writer you are – a 'plotter' or a 'pantser,' or somewhere in-between?

UNDERSTANDING WHAT TYPE OF WRITER YOU ARE ON THE PLOTTER TO PANSTER SCALE

A plotter believes in a plan, an outline before writing their novels, like J.K Rowling or Ernest Hemingway. Pantsers belong to the other extreme. They do not have a plan; the term 'pantser' refers to flying by the seat of their pants. Literary giants like Margaret Atwood and Stephen King belong to this category, proving that there's no one path to creative success, but each works for the respective writer.

When planning your book for the first time, it is crucial to understand whether you are a plotter or a pantser. Most writers will be somewhere between the two extremes but knowing where you fall on the scale before writing is good to know. There are several intermediate stages, from meticulous detail-oriented plotters to a go-with-the-creative-flow pantser. Let's try to understand each with the metaphor of the gardener, the architect, the designer, and the knitter.

The gardener sows the seed and waits for the plant to grow to take its course of life. They know not how many branches, flowers, or kinds of leaves will grow. This category of writer believes in the organic growth of events and incidents through the storyline. They do not care for a well-drawn outline. Our pantsers fall under this category.

But the architect always proceeds with a detailed blueprint. They know which window will be found in which part of the house even before building it. Such writers are the plotters.

Designers stand somewhere between. They have a pencil sketch ready and a vision of how the final painting will look, but no set color scheme. They let it shape up along the way. This category of writers likes to begin with a rough skeleton and keep adding flesh and blood to it as the story proceeds. They have a plan to start with but let the narrative take its course hinged on that plan.

The knitters are yet another extreme. They sit and write as the scenes pop into their imagination and do a lot of reverse engineering to weave the threads together. It's like filling in the blanks as they write. An outline will be helpful for them as long as they can go back and forth in moving the scenes around.

First, you must identify if you are a "plotter" or a "pantser," an architect, or a gardener. A plotter will go slower than their pantser counterparts and stick to a rigid schedule while writing the book. While the other two categories, the designer and the knitter, have different approaches to outlining. Naturally, each one will have a different creative journey. So before deciding how your outline should be written, you need to have a clear vision of what kind of a writer you are. For example, are you somebody who will start with an idea and let it spread wings as the plot unfolds, or do you want to begin from a point where you know exactly how your protagonist will die or live happily ever after? Or are you someone who has thought out the childhood and wedding scene but is yet to find a way to introduce the love interest in the character's life? Once you know your writer type, you will know the best-suited method to write a book outline.

Since writing is a highly subjective creative endeavor, every writer's work bears a stamp of their personality. Knowing your writer's personality helps you make the best choice of the method that aligns with your creative process. The best method is the method that best suits your temperament. In these chapters, I will introduce you to several book outlining strategies dictated by different writer personalities.

2

DIFFERENT TYPES OF OUTLINES TO CHOOSE FROM

So what's your method for writing a book outline? In the last chapter, I discussed how you need first to identify your writer category, where you fit in on the pantser to plotter scale. Once you know where you stand, you can improve your methods, and book outlining becomes easier. It can be from a fifty-page, fully detailed document to a short, bulleted list. All you need to ensure is that it answers the three critical questions mentioned earlier:

- What is the main takeaway for the reader from the story? (This can be from a profound life lesson to just reminding the reader to live in the moment)
- What timeline, pressures, and challenges are working on your characters? (Pressure must be injected into a story to bring excitement into it)

- What's at stake for the characters, and how do they develop under these pressures as the narrative proceeds? (The main character must have something important to lose or to gain to drive them to the next scene)

Besides answering these humongous questions, a good book outline will achieve three more things crucial to your book's success: it gives you a big picture, enables you to organize the big and small details, and allows your creativity to shine. However, some feel outlining has a stifling influence on creativity, but that's a different discussion altogether. How rigid or flexible your outlining method is, the organization of your content mustn't be at the cost of creativity.

There are many ways to organize your book, and they all have something in common. This guide will show you what they are and which kinds you should use. If you don't want to use one of the more advanced ones because it seems more work and may not help that much, then don't use them right away, but it's always good to have some plan or structure in place.

Remember, the human brain can't concentrate on multiple ideas at once, so having those ideas written down in order can only help with clarity of thought.

I will briefly discuss these other methods, but I will later focus on the technique I use, and we can build an outline together as a small project to start you off.

THE SNOWFLAKE METHOD

The snowflake method is probably the most respected method used to plan and outline a novel. The originator of this method, Randy Ingermanson, is a theoretical physicist, award winning novelist, and fiction teacher. The procedure is based on the most straightforward ideas and then building outwards on the same idea. Ingermanson's methodology is a simple premise that a novel cannot be conjured out of thin air or pulled out like a magician's hat rabbit. It has to be designed incrementally. The idea is to start with one basic story idea or deep theme and then keep growing it, you add layers of complexities and resolutions until you have a full-blown novel.

This method creates a story from a small idea; it may not be suitable if the concept is already in your mind.

The snowflake method gives us a ten-step design principle, taking one step at a time. The writer starts with one sentence about the story and, from there, a paragraph with the setup of the account, then three turning points, and then the conclusion – five sentences. The next stage is character development and then expanding on each sentence in the paragraph. There are ten steps, and let's consider each step sequentially:

1. One sentence summary: This should be your novel in a nutshell, like "an orphan boy discovers he is a wizard and goes to the best school of magic to learn where he learns who killed his parents and how." Do not use any character names or further details that will be covered in the following steps.

2. Sentence to paragraph: Elaborate the sentence into a paragraph adding additional significant information. The best way to expand is to add setup elements, three major plot points or turning points in the story, and a conclusion. This technique will give you a rough structure of the story and better clarity on the role your characters would play. It would be best if you didn't move on to the next step until you have accomplished this.

3. Character development: Now write a one-paragraph summary of your major characters' journeys based on their storyline, motivations, and goals (what they are chasing abstractly and concretely or what do they want and what do they need), conflict (what hinders them from achieving those goals), epiphany (what do they realize or learn). Developing characters is a vital step, and you must spend a few hours in this process.

4. Expand the summary paragraph: Follow the process to step two and expand each sentence into a paragraph, a process that can be time-consuming. To quote Randy, "Take several hours and expand each sentence of your summary paragraph into a full paragraph. All but the last paragraph should end in a disaster. The final paragraph should tell how the book ends."

5. Detailed character outline: Take each character outline you made in step three and expand it into a one-page description where the characters tell their story from their viewpoint. In this step, you identify and resolve any issues with character motivation.

6. Expand the one-page summary: Go back to step four and expand the one-page book summary exponentially into a four-page synopsis. This last step is a crucial step where you identify the plot holes and loose ends.

7. Develop complete character charts: Build on step five and draw out a full-fledged character chart with these details:

- Birthdate
- Physical description
- Back story
- Motives
- Life goals

8. List the scenes: helped by the extended synopsis, chart out the list of scenes that will make your novel's narrative. A classic book has between fifty to a hundred of these scenes.

9. Scene description: Use the scene list to expand each scene into a multi-paragraph narrative description. You must include these two descriptions: a list of characters appearing and a detailed description of what happens in the stages.

10. Start writing: Now you have enough material to write the first draft, so how would you feel about using this technique?

THE AGENDA METHOD

The idea behind this system is that it's character-driven; you allow your main protagonist's actions to build your story. So it would help if you start by putting yourself in your protagonists' shoes. Track the main characters' journey as they and the narrative progress and start keeping notes thinking like the character. This method helps you see your characters' schedule and motivations, quests, and predicaments and respond to situations as they would as the plot proceeds. This technique means that your characters will still have reasons even if they aren't precisely defined so things are more accessible for you when writing them down later on.

It would help if you took notes as it goes along, so don't forget about anything important. Even if you forget something, you will have a good idea of what your characters do every time something happens. You can jot down scribblings, bullet points, or even drawings. Once and a while, you can organize the notes and see how the plot/character develops. While taking notes, you don't have to write them down in a definite order; put them wherever makes sense to your characters' journey.

Ensure that your characters are consistent and stay the same throughout the book. Make sure their motivations and goals remain constant throughout the narrative, and their responses are appropriate and authentic to the character in every crisis/situation.

THE BOOKEND METHOD

This outlining method is widely used in magazines, novels, and screenwriting for a seamless plot structure. In the bookend technique, the writer should begin with creating two bookends: the first and the last one. The first bookend should be in an anecdote involving the characters and actions in line with the book's central idea (the main plot). The final bookend is the resolution or conclusion to the first bookend. Once you fill the story between, there's a logical flow of the narrative that forms the body of the novel.

The logic behind the bookend technique is simple: once you know where you start from and where you are headed, you will not lose your way. It is a sound organizing principle for your writing, as you already have a clear sense of getting closure to your narrative.

THE BEAT METHOD

The Beat method is a comprehensive and accurate way of outlining your novel. The trick is to divide the beginning, middle, and end into 15 beats or main points. Each point or beat pertains to the overarching structure of your novel. By breaking down the story in this fashion, you get a clear idea of word count and which part requires more or fewer words than others.

The Beat method, also known as Blake Snyder's 'Save the Cat! Beat Sheet' proceeds in stages. First, you must divide your target word count into three acts, comprising 25%, 50%, and 25% of your total narrative. Then, divide each act into a target number of scenes, and based on the word count in each scene, you can figure out how many scenes you will write in all. Each scene's magic number of words runs between 1000 to 2000 words. Based on this figure and the percentage of word count in each of the three acts, you can easily calculate the total number of scenes.

We come to the most crucial stage – determining where each of the 15 story beats goes based on the scene division. As per Blake Snyder's formula, here are the 15 story points:

1. Opening image – 1%
2. Statement of theme – 5%
3. Setup – 1-10%
4. Catalyst – 10%
5. Debate – 10% -20%
6. Break Into Two – 20%
7. B Story – 22%

8. Fun and Games – 20% - 50%
9. Midpoint – 50%
10. Bad Guys Close In – 50% -75%
11. All is Lost – 75%
12. Dark Night of the Soul – 75% to 80%
13. Break Into Three – 80%
14. Finale – 80% - 99%
15. Final Image – 99% - 100%

Here's the journey from the opening image to the final image with a tentative percentage wise division, but do not get overwhelmed by the numbers; they are not as daunting as they appear to be. It's just a formula to figure out how much of the total word count goes into which story point. So once you have the bigger picture sorted, the rest of the word count division will fall in place.

Now the question is, what should be the standard word count for a novel? A usual rounds up to anything between 80,000-100,000 words. Though I believe anything over 40,000 words falls into a novel category, 50,000 is regarded as the minimum novel length. Finding your way through the beat sheet will be easier with these ballpark estimates.

THE THREE ACTS METHOD

The three acts method has been there forever as a structuring principle for outlining novels, perhaps even before it was named. It gives the background and sets the stage for your characters to act and respond to each other's conflicting motives. The three acts are the setup, the confrontation, and the resolution. The first act needs an introduction to the characters, their everyday lives, and the lead-up to the story conflict. The second act is the event that throws the protagonist into the unexpected and removes them from the comfort of the first act. Here you introduce other vital characters that will play a significant role in your book and introduce major crises and hurdles in your main character's journey. The third act will lead to the climax of the conflict and explain the competition and the resolution. This third act is where everything comes together and gets resolved, leaving no loose ends or unanswered questions.

The three-act method is a complete way of storytelling as it divides the narratives into three levels, mapping to the readers' desires or expectations from every story.

THE TREE METHOD

The tree method suits the gardener writer looking for a better structure. The tree method can be divided into three parts: the basic idea, the main plot, and the details. Think of the seed as the initial story idea. As the tree grows, the trunk becomes more robust, like the story's central plot, as more detail is added. Branches that extend off the tree can be characters, character developments, plot twists, conflicts, subplots, etc.

It is an incremental and developmental method in which you start from scratch, the basic idea, and then the plot thickens as the adage goes! The story progresses, and the details grow out of and around the main plot organically. This book outline leaves a lot of room for creativity and organic growth of the narrative.

THE SYNOPSIS METHOD

A synopsis is a simple document, just a page or two, that provides a quick overview of what your book will look like. This overview doesn't have to be fancy or detailed; it just needs to tell you what's going on in the book, the crux of your story. It's a rough explanation of what happens in the book, including the major points, the beginning, middle, end, the conflicts, and the resolution. This summary allows the writer to see where the story is going but with plenty of room for flexibility.

You can also include this with your query letter when you're sending it out so people can get a better idea of what it's about before they request it.

THE IN-DEPTH METHOD

To make your story as good as possible and see it has no holes or problems you might overlook later, then the in-depth method will help. The opposite of the Synopsis method involves pages of notes with every detail of the plot, characters, and scenes. J.K. Rowling has impressive handwritten outlines with this method. Her *Harry Potter* series is based on her detailed handwritten outlines with columns representing the book's timeline and tracking the characters' journey.

The in-depth method does take a lot of time as it is a comprehensive outlining method involving writing chapter summaries and scene outlines within those chapters. But when you fall back on it while writing, the actual writing process becomes much easier and less time consuming.

THE BULLETED METHOD

This method is a straightforward way to do things, and it's also a good way for beginners to learn about writing. The reason is simple – creating a bulleted list is not rocket science. So if outlining methods feels slightly overwhelming as a new writer, go for the classic note-taking device of writing down bullet points. The idea is to create a bulleted list containing the most critical moments in a book, whether related to the plot or the character. It is a quick fix to your outlining needs – the moment something essential strikes, put down a bulleted list without losing the train of thoughts. It is compact and to the point, just a list of crucial details on which you can build the narrative. The list can also act as a checklist for self-reviewing the first draft.

THE EXCEL METHOD

For the tech-savvy (and even the non-tech-savvy), a simple spreadsheet with columns for scene description, characters, setting, plots, and subplots can be an ideal organizing principle. This method gives you room for copying and pasting rows to create a perfect timeline. This is more of a technique for people writing more than one book or a multi-book novel series. If you're only planning on writing one book and are not a big fan of technology, you might want to skip this method.

If you are planning on making your novel a series, this is the best way to organize it. One way to do it is to create an Excel spreadsheet with two columns called Spoilers and Plot Twists. In the first column, write down all the spoilers about your book and what's going on with your characters.

The Plot Twists column lists the different plot points, twists, and turns leading to the climax. This method will help keep your plot engaging for the readers, avoid confusion and identify plot holes early.

It will help if you add a character sheet to write down information about each of your characters and a column for the timeline. This will give you an overall sense of form at a glance.

THE VISUAL METHOD

This is mainly for people planning on writing a series. This method aims to literally draw out the events and the people involved in them in a comic book style. Color-coded flashcards or Post-its, each containing a sentence related to the story. This is ideal for those who have jumbled up ideas and need to visualize them to get them into a logical order. This resource resembles a landscape of Post-it notes. J.K. Rowling's handwritten outline was also a kind of visual outlining.

This can be a great way to get your ideas out on paper and make sure that everything is planned out so it doesn't look like a mess. It gives you a panoramic view of your work and its look and feel, which helps you do any major or minor quick fixes required at an early stage of outlining.

The best thing about this method is that it's not a one-time thing but a flexible outlining approach where you can keep trying different combinations and make changes as you proceed. This method works best for both the designer and knitter type of writers.

These are colorful collections of book outlining methods you can pick and choose from. However, which one works for you and which doesn't is yours to work out. A book outlining approach is no guaranteed formula for creativity; it's an organizing principle to give your imagination a proper direction. Hence blindly trusting one method as the formula for successful outlining may not lead you anywhere unless you have that creativity. The technique will only fan your creativity and inspire organizational skills.

To some writers, character building promotes creativity and sparks the imagination; hence starting with character outlining can be a good idea. To others devising the plot can be a better breeding ground for character building. Also, where to begin your organization is one big question that can never have one good answer. In the next chapter, I will discuss how to develop the plot and investigate plot holes. Before we get to that, I will show you how I now do my outlines; get yourself in front of a PC or Mac and allow me to walk you through it.

THE JOHN S. WARNER METHOD

My method is an assortment of ideas snatched from more experienced writers and sprinkled with some of my preferences. It makes perfect sense to me and might to you once I've explained how it works.

Start with a Google Drive spreadsheet; they are free and can be found by searching Google sheets; you may need an account. Let's do it together and work through it step by step: I will start by using the premise of one of my old stories under another pen name; it's an excellent story to help you grip the technique.

Step 1.

Open the sheet and rename it "Time Travel Book Outline." The sheet has A to Z across the top and numbers down the left-hand side, The letters are your columns, and the numbers are your rows.

Step 2.

Name the columns at the top with these headings in this order: Day, Date, Chapter Name, Plot, Location, Weather, and then your name as a heading (you are the protagonist in this story, and you're about to travel through time).

Step 3.

Underneath these headings, put today's Day and Date and call the chapter "The Argument." I like to link the weather or location with the feel of the mood in the scene. Mark the weather column as "Windy." Under the plot heading, write, "Have a blazing row with my partner after being called selfish and leave the house to clear my head with a walk."

Step 4.

Time to use your imagination; name the chapter "The Anomaly" and use the same day and date but name the location where you may walk in these circumstances (Somewhere isolated and quiet). Each row is a scene, and each column tells you information about the scene. In this scene, work out a way for your character to travel accidentally through a Time hole and arrive two years after your birth.

Step 5.

Now, being trapped in another time with no money, house, or friends, what will you do? You know of future events; you have your mobile phone, but how will this help you? Start thinking of how the story may progress and add information. Include scenes with dates on your google sheet; if new important characters appear, give them a heading on your sheet. Try advancing the tale and see how using the sheet will help you visualize and make a focused narrative. Add color to different characters or locations. Notice you can drag and drop rows and columns into various positions to tailor your story as new scenes come to you. Using this technique, it's elementary to add information to a scene, just add a new column and put the info on the correct date.

Step 6.

Once I have all the scenes I need, I then use the beat method mentioned earlier in this chapter to mold the scenes into the correct structure; this will involve culling some scenes and swapping some around; I also try to get a good balance of different characters perspectives in each chapter, which can make for a more exciting read especially if you leave each scene on a cliff hanger.

Step 7.

Build on your story by adding details, characters or other events. I jot down ideas on Post-it notes which I keep in a box. Every few days, I expand them and add them to the google sheet or get rid of them. It's not a fast process, but it's a good one.

3

DEVELOPING A PLOT AND FILLING PLOT HOLES WITH WHAT IFS

Once you have an outline, it's easy to develop the plotline. However, a gripping plot requires identifying the plot holes and filling them early, for starters. This chapter will discuss how to evolve an engaging plot and address or fill the plot holes to keep it casual, logical, and organic. But before going deep into the technique, let's consider the essential plot elements which your book outline must cover if you wish to write a captivating plot.

8 Plot Elements Your Outline Needs

1. Story Goal

To have a clear story goal start with asking this question: what is the problem that must be solved or the goal that must be achieved. You need to know what is happening with the main character, why they are going through so much trouble. The main character wants something serious and worth having for them; hence, they go through many risks and cross many hurdles. Any story's plot should include incidents and events where the main character is solving a problem or attaining a goal. The problem your protagonist attempts to solve or the purpose they aspire to reach should affect or involve most of the other characters in the story. This is how you interweave the different characters' journeys, motivations, and interests to create and resolve complications in the plot.

2. The Consequence

Once you have decided on the story goal, ask the following question: what happens if the goal is not met or the problem is not solved? What are the consequences your protagonist worries about if they fail to solve the problem or achieve the desired goal?

Thinking about this helps you conjure up scenarios and complications which can deter your protagonist's journey towards achieving the goal. The consequence is a negative situation that might occur when the goal is not met, making the solution more meaningful and challenging for the character. It can be introduced in two ways. First, the protagonist sets their mind to a goal or a problem to solve. Then eventually, when they learn of the consequences, the fear of failure makes the goal more important. Another way to introduce the consequence is to show the character threatened by the result, and this fear of failure motivates them to find a way to solve the problem. According to Melanie Phelps, in some stories, the consequence is already in effect in the beginning. For example, in *Back to the Future*, Marty has to get his young parents to fall in love, or he will cease to exist. This is not a choice; it's something he has to do to live, so his motivations are strong.

In all the cases, fear of failure is the dominant driving force for the characters to act and react. Hence, a combination of goal and consequence creates the dramatic tension, and the characters' predicament gives them a direction to follow. Without this, your story will have no definite purpose and will stop being interesting. What can you write about a protagonist who has everything they need and doesn't want to go anywhere?

3. Requirements

Now that you know what your character is pursuing and what happens if they fail, you need to answer the following important question: how do they fix the problem or meet their goal? You need to think about all the requirements, everything necessary for your character to do or go through to reach their destination. Think of these essentials as a checklist or even different video game levels. The reader will look forward to how the protagonist passes each level to reach the desired goal. While ticking off each element in that checklist, the readers' anticipation, excitement, and participation in the story grow. To create your list of requirements, you need to consider all the possibilities and likelihoods to lead the character to their final goal.

4. Forewarnings

If you want your book to work, you must add some edgy element that keeps the reader biting their nails. The best way to ensure your reader is involved in your character's journey is by including some forewarning – events that make the reader cringe as a consequence is approaching. These forewarnings are a considerable part of your outline because it gives a certain sense of anxiety and nervousness you rarely get in real life. Your readers will try and anticipate what's coming before it happens, and it's a great feeling because they won't be able to wait until they're done reading the story.

Forewarnings and requirements balance out each other. While requirements take your character one step closer to the desired goals, forewarnings are signs they might not complete the task. Just like the tussle between goals and consequences creates dramatic tension, the opposing forces of requirements and forewarnings fire the reader's emotional tension and involvement in your book as they are kept hanging between hope and disappointment. The reader by no means can afford to put the book down until they discover which way the ball will roll.

5. Costs

As they say, nothing worth having comes easy; if what your character seeks comes easy, then it's not something to be prized. Instead, the goal should be something serious, something of lasting value to them to achieve, which they have to pay a hefty price in terms of the struggles they encounter, the hurdles they pass, the choices, and the sacrifices they make. The higher the stakes, the graver the sacrifice, the worthier the goal! This is the golden rule of plot development – raise the stakes for your character so they emerge as extraordinary for pursuing something worthy for them.

The price your protagonist has to pay can be in any form, a material sacrifice, physical pain, and suffering, or giving up on something abstract like their self-respect, pride, honor, love, a way of life, or the life of a dear one, etc. The harder the sacrifice for the protagonist, the more deserving they become of the goal in the readers' eyes. This helps the readers establish empathy with the character.

6. Dividends

The costs are balanced by the dividends – the rewards the character achieves on their way to fulfilling the goal. These rewards are unrelated to the bigger picture, the desired goal; neither are these essential milestones, like the requirements, to reach the destination. Instead, these are added incentives that your character would never have received if they hadn't tried to achieve the goal in the first place.

7. Prerequisites

Another vital question is what must happen for the requirements to occur? Prerequisites are events that lead you to the requirements and hence one step closer to the goal. Let's try to understand with an example. In *Harry Potter and the Philosopher's Stone*, Harry must get the philosopher's stone, but to reach it, he must play and win the wizard chess. This is a requirement, the prerequisite is that Harry must know how to play wizard chess, and earlier in the story, we see Ron and Harry playing wizard chess.

List possible accomplishments your protagonist must have before meeting the requirements to achieve their goal. This list is the list of prerequisites.

8. Preconditions

Preconditions are minor versions of the forewarnings. They are minor impediments that stall the character's path to happiness. There are many ways these can be imposed, but primarily it's done by other characters. For instance, Lydia Languish, in Sheridan's play *The Rivals* wants a complicated love story; she wants to marry beneath her class so her aunt opposes the match. Hence, our well-off hero Anthony poses as a less fortunate young man to court Lydia. This imposition by Lydia is a minor impediment in Anthony's pursuit of love.

BUILDING AN OUTLINE WITH WHAT IFS

"What if a wealthy, unmarried man gets acquainted with a family of five unmarried daughters?" results in *Pride and Prejudice*. "What if a baby wizard survived a killing curse?" The result is the seven-book series of the *Harry Potter* novels. 'What if there was an entirely fantastical world down the rabbit hole in your garden?" and the outcome is Alice in Wonderland.

All great literature begins with one 'what if' question. 'What ifs' are an excellent brainstorming tool. Write down all your questions about your plot, don't censor your questions; no idea is too stupid at this stage. Let's use an example of this Invisible man story.

- What if the hero gets into a radiation accident and becomes invisible?
- What if the antagonist convinces his girlfriend he disappeared because he doesn't want to marry her?
- What if she believes him and breaks off the engagement?
- What if the invisible man finds the formula to regain his visible form but has to steal it from his best friend, the scientist's office?
- What if this jeopardizes the scientist's job, and the hero loses his friendship forever?
- What if he chooses to remain invisible? How will he feel to see the competitor stealing his girlfriend?

- What if he enjoys the power that comes with invisibility?
- What if he loses his family and property rights for having absconded? These are just a few scenarios, and all these questions pop out as plot possibilities.

List such what-if questions, and for each what if, list as many possible outcomes. Take each outcome and develop the idea a little more. Continuing with the present example, the possibilities can be:

- The man finds the formula
- He learns how to apply it
- He comes back to visible form
- He saves his family's wealth and his love

Choose the outcomes you like. And begin the process again for each development. Now you go deeper into the process and weigh the counter possibilities: What if the man chooses not to come back to a visible form? This would end the story and hence be discarded, but obviously, it can act as a moment of inner conflict for the character when he finally chooses.

Consider the list with a fresh pair of eyes and choose what flows best with your core what-if question and resolution possibilities. Finally, you have a basic plotline ready!

HOW TO FILL THOSE ANNOYING PLOT HOLES

Once you have a rough sketch of the plotline, it's easy to identify the cavities in your story, what we call the plot holes. Your account is probably filled with plot holes, and it's something that you might not want to think about at this stage. You might like these gaps to be filled organically during the writing process. But guess what, these gaping gaps can lead to a dead-end, a writer's block.

So, how to identify and address plot holes at this nascent stage of plot development? Start with asking yourself what you don't know or aren't sure of in terms of

- Character motivations
- Filler scenes
- Character relationships

Continuing with the example of our invisible man, try to understand why he does not want to regain his visible form? What is holding him back? What is making him pursue a solution? Then look for the filler scenes. What is contributing to a continuous narrative flow? Where are the glitches, and what can you do to make the narrative flow more seamless? Finally, consider the intermingled motivations: what if your invisible hero regains visible shape? Who will be most unhappy? What will they possibly do to keep him from returning to visible form?

The process often leads to a list of problems. Rather than focusing on the issues, it would be best if you turned them into questions so you can look for solutions. Again, answer the questions with what-ifs and explore the outcomes.

SHOULD SUBPLOTS BE OUTLINED?

During the what-if brainstorming, you might come across several ideas that may not be brilliant enough to contribute to the main plot. There's no need to discard all of them as they can be excellent subplot material if you try to develop them in terms of:

- Minor characters' motivations
- Their relationships with significant characters
- Their relationships with other minor characters

In our example, the scientist's friend and the hero's mother are essential subplot elements. Try to ask a few questions regarding their motivations, their relationships with the hero, his love interest, and the antagonist. These questions will give you a lot of clarity about creating interwoven character tracks and allow you space to develop other interesting minor characters. Do not discard any idea before penning it down. Instead, try to streamline the subplot elements once you finish the list with similar what-if questions as you created for the main plot. See what contributes most to the main story and what is superfluous. Remember, plot development is not just about what to keep; it's more about what to discard.

Organization is the key to efficient plot outlining. You can be a pen and paper writer or tech savvy one click-clacking on the computer. Whatever form of scribbling you follow, use a color-coding pattern. This helps segregate the best, mediocre and redundant ideas highlighted in different color codes so you can adeptly pick and choose.

4

MAKING SENSE OF THE SETTING AND TIMELINE

Think like a reader – what strikes you most about a book? Most of us would agree that one or more characters stand out and appeal to our imagination; in some books, it's the location or settings that capture our minds. Like JK Rowling's Hogwarts or in R.K. Narayan's collection Malgudi Days, we meet many characters who stand out, but besides the characters, we remember most vividly Malgudi. Malgudi, the fictional Indian smalltown from the 1930s, is the most memorable character per se. You can almost smell and taste the town through its description. Many novelists create imaginary locales that cannot be found on the map but are highly relatable, like the Yoknapatawpha county of William Faulkner or Thomas Hardy's Egdon Heath. What do these writers do differently that makes the setting stand out rather than outshine the characterization? We will get to that shortly.

Another significant aspect is the timeline. In Emily Bronte's Wuthering Heights, the narrative covers the events of three decades, and unless Bronte had a drawn-out timeline, she wouldn't have put together such a gripping tale of love and loss across time. To make the action engaging, you must have complete control over time and place, and once you set the setting and timeline straight in your outline, you will have full control over the narrative flow.

UNDERSTANDING THE SETTING AND TIMELINE

The setting is the period and geographical location of the story. It is the backdrop against which the action of the novel unfolds. It can include culture and historical periods. Typically, they are natural, cultural, historical, or public/private places. Let us try to understand each type of setting with famous literary examples.

1. **Culture or Historical:** When the human story of the novel unfolds against a particular cultural or historical milieu, the setting can influence the character's destiny and dictates their actions. We all are familiar with Charles Dickens's *A Tale of Two Cities*. It is a historical novel, the activity of which oscillates between two cities, London and Paris, between 1755 and 1793, amid the momentous events

of European history. It was the time before and during the French Revolution. The story of love is enacted against the socio-cultural backdrop of the conditions leading to the French Revolution and its aftermath, as the social hierarchy was upturned and the Reign of Terror began. Similarly, Ernest Hemingway's *A Farewell to Arms* is set during the Italian campaign of World War I. Last but not least, Narayan's short story collection *Malgudi Days* is set in a fictional South Indian town Malgudi, going through a change in culture and social life from the 1930s to the 1960s in newly independent India.

2. **Natural:** In some novels, nature becomes a powerful force against which the human struggle is dramatized. We all are familiar with Nobel laureate William Golding's *Lord of the Flies*. The natural setting plays a crucial role in unmasking the primitive self of the group of schoolboys once they find themselves on a deserted island free from social restraint and restrictions. Another classic is Daniel Defoe's *Robinson Crusoe*, the story of the survival and success of a man marooned after a shipwreck on a deserted island. Nature plays an intriguing and life-changing role in Yann Martel's *Life of Pi* protagonist. The novel's main action takes place on the open sea as a boy and a tiger are codependent for survival on a lifeboat, fighting against nature, hunger, and instincts.

3. **Public/Private:** The public and the private world can be significant settings in novels. Examples of a private setting include Bram Stoker's Dracula, where we see Jonathan Harker's struggle set against the backdrop of the count's castle filled with some highly upsetting surprises for him. Then later in the novel, the setting changes to Whitby and a public location in the quaint British seaside town.

There are several other settings like fantasy, imaginary, dream, dystopian, utopian, mythical/mythological, alternative reality, sci-fi, post-apocalyptic, etc. These are the broad types of settings. The secret to writing a successful novel is understanding your location and creating a workable logic on which the universe of your novel functions. For example, Hogwarts is no real school of magic, but J.K. Rowling's narrative is so convincing that we do not for a moment question the rationale behind the school House teams playing a match of Quidditch (no football or cricket) flying on their brooms.

Coming to the timeline, it is the chronology of the events in your novel. The timescale depends on the events in a timeline. For example, war can last for years; a battle is a timescale that occurs within the timeline. The timeline decides the arrangement and order of events to streamline your characters' journey; it allows you to incorporate events that are duration-wise most likely to have happened during the entire span of your novel. It gives a certain continuity to the plot, as you do not want to miss out on the events that happened within your character's life that may bear some impact on their present state. The timeline answers questions like:

- Why and when does the story start?
- When does it end?
- How old are your characters when the story begins?
- How old are they when the story ends?
- When do they meet other people (characters) as the story unfolds?

The timeline can be linear or nonlinear, depending on what kind of action your novel covers. If it is too psychological, the character's mind can go back and forth in time. Hence, the writer must be extra cautious in sticking to the timeline so the details do not go haywire and confuse the reader.

CREATING A VIVID SETTING

The first task is the place, which has to match the plot's pace. It can be any geographical location or the immediate surroundings, but does it match the story's mood. The place can be an essential tool to communicate the character's perspective, temperament, disposition, and predicament. For instance, to create a sense of urgency, the character will not be on a beach; they will be on a busy street, driving during the rush hours. So you'll set them up in a public place on a busy Monday morning, not strolling along the sidewalk later in the evening.

Decide on how to describe the time. It can be a time of the day or a season of the year. Different time and place settings always correspond to the character's mood and action. The first caffeine rush of the day puts the character in the morning while falling leaves and a nip in the air set the stage for Fall. Imagine the impact a funeral scene set on a day with an overcast sky and rain can have on the reader. And then, after the service is over, you show the recently widowed character walking away. The rain stopped now, and from behind the clouds, a sliver of sunlight peeks as the woman looks up. This time place setting conveys a whole sequence of emotions, the character's journey from despair to hope, present loss to the days in the future looking bright in just one scene, expressed purely through the setting.

Another crucial time element is historical periodization. We already discussed a few examples above about historical settings in famous literary works. A time in history dictates a lot of the character portrayal, their proper actions and personal attitudes, the social attitudes, and the entire cultural milieu where the human drama unfolds. Therefore, the writer must be consistent and particular about the detailing while portraying a historical period for authenticity.

The next significant step to bringing your novel's world to life through vivid detailing is to put yourself in the character's shoes. It's like a child who loves Mickey Mouse but is terrified when they see the character at Disneyland. It's not until you get down to the child's level that you can see how big Mickey actually is. Remember, you are writing the story, but your characters are living it. Naturally, to make their world more dynamic and vivid, you must see it from their viewpoint. Let the layers unfold as the character lives their story. Close research is essential for vivid detailing, but too many nitty-gritty, over-detailing descriptions can be overkill for the reader. The most appealing setting descriptions come from the character's eye, which is allowed to miss out on some details and see the world slightly altered from how it originally was.

One vital aspect of creating your setting that should not be lost sight of is that it must have a dynamic relationship with the characters. The characters animate the location by inhabiting it; in its turn, the setting influences the characters' lives. The best example is seen in Thomas Hardy's *Return of the Native*, where the location, Egdon Heath, becomes a character itself. The heath's impact on an ambitious woman like Bathsheba Everdene, driving her to the extent of trying to escape it and ultimately her death, is noteworthy. Ideally you want a philosophical impact from the setting onto the character's psyche, their moods or mental state to bring the scene to life.

Now that you know the 'what' of creating engaging settings, let's focus on the how. There are some simple exercises you could do.

- Try visiting an actual location and absorb its essence. It should be a real place near you or a particular area that's already been described in a novel if you are lucky enough to live near one. Focus on the sensory experience – the sights, sounds, and smells. Once you are back at your desk, relive that experience and jot it down or check the novel to see if the experience matched the description.
- Select a location and try placing two characters from your book in that place. Write a conversation between them based on how they will respond to this setting.
- Keep the details of your locale accurate to the character's sensory abstract experience instead of the vivid concrete descriptions. Remember, the character's experience brings the setting to life.
- It helps if you could make it more graphic, like creating a map of your world on a blank page. Attention to detail is crucial – mark the significant landforms and more minor landmarks, like a statue on the head of the street, a bakery down the alley, the library on the next block, etc. This should get you to think about location more when writing fiction.

HOW TO ORGANIZE YOUR TIMELINE

Timelines are good for plotting time-sensitive events. For example, there is no sense in a pregnant character experiencing winter followed by another winter. It helps determine the order of appearance of certain characters and the opportune moment for their backstory revelation. A timeline gives background information on a character, plan character motivations, and group objects and places. This helps you determine the information flow throughout the story – how much to reveal at which point. If you prefer the visual method of outlining in flashcards and Post-its and playing around with the order, timelining can work for you just right for trying out different combinations.

Create a timeline for the story, plus a timeline for each main character. This will help with the viewpoint of the different characters. Visual techniques are convenient. Flashcards, spreadsheets, drop and drag software, or timeline software can help. I use the John Warner method but the up-and-coming writers of this age can bank on some helpful planning tools like Scrivener and Scapple. Scrivener is a long-form writing tool with three significant features:

- A binder sidebar that lets you organize your chapters and scenes; you can color code and drag and drop to rearrange
- A corkboard to scribble your ideas, scenes, locations, and characters
- An outliner view with synopsis and word count

Scapple, the close cousin of Scrivener, helps you in mind mapping your ideas. Another tool called Xmind aids you in doing everything from free-form mind mapping to timelining your novel. It also comes in handy for making organizational charts and character relationship diagrams. To create a story outline with complete character, location, and story arcs on a panoramic timeline view, then Aeon Timeline could be the tool you need. It is an effective way to track the timeline for writing novels on an epic or historical scale. Writers also find Trello a helpful organizing tool, especially for character planning. I haven't tried any of the software mentioned above but have read some reviews and looked into the software, and I could hardly advise on writing if I didn't mention other options available to a writer.

HOW MICHAEL CRICHTON CREATED A TIMELINE WITH PLOT CARDS

Even for those born with a natural flair for writing, planning and organizing your material can be challenging. For those struggling with keeping it organized, famous author, screenwriter, and director Michael Chrichton's method for plotting a story can be a go-to technique to fall back on. Crichton is one of those rare personalities to have earned the unique distinction of having the number one film *Jurassic Park*, the number one TV show *ER*, and the number one book *Disclosure*, all in 1994. So how could he possibly do it?

Before writing a single word, Crichton took 3" x 5" index cards with him to Harvard Medical School while studying there. He kept them in his pocket and jotted down ideas as they came to him. He would use various cards and staple them together for a sequence of ideas. At the end of the day, he put them all in a shoebox and replaced the used cards with a fresh blank set. When the box was full or he had no more ideas, he would walk away for some time. Then, he would take all the cards, spread them out into the timeline, and put the ordered cards into an index-card box. He would spend a few days adding ideas where he deemed fit. He took the first index card and wrote the first paragraph when he was ready.

Since writing is 90% thinking and 10% jotting down the story on the page, this method can help you keep your thinking cap on without losing significant ideas. Once you have enough, you can spend more time refining and editing your train of thought by adding new cards or reordering the existing sequences. The thinking and ideation part might not be as exciting as developing characters and the plot. Still, it is an essential part of a novel's outline because it will iron out any potential issues that could hinder the reader's understanding or, worse, enjoyment. Better to address the hiccups at the inception than to get stuck halfway through your writing.

5

GROWING CHARACTERS THAT CAPTIVATE THE READERS

There's one golden rule of character development that every writer must pay attention to – do not tell your reader everything you know about your characters. Consider this: if a reader knows everything about a character, it is easy to figure out how they will behave in a situation. Their reactions, responses, choices, and ultimately, destiny will be too evident to the reader. This element of predictability mars the engagement level of the reader by spoiling the element of surprise. Some writers prefer only to let the reader know 10% of what the writer knows about the character. No matter how much you wish to reveal or conceal your characters from your readers, it would help if you were clear about the specifics of each one of them.

WHAT DOES A WRITER NEED TO KNOW ABOUT THEIR CHARACTERS?

I find character development the most interesting part of a novel outlining journey. In fact I've written two books prior to this on the secrets to creating character arcs so you could say I'm more than interested. This is where your creativity can have a free hand to play around with attributes, physical, mental, social, emotional, cultural, and psychological. Each character is a complete person you get to create from scratch. Start with the exterior details and then make your way inside the life and mind of the characters. Let's make a precise character development itinerary to make your job easier at the outlining phase:

1. **External traits**- External traits are physical attributes and features. Your characters' appearance, accent, health, accessories, and props come under this category. In this part, you can provide your characters with a remarkable physical attribute or trait that reflects or can be a metaphor for their temperament or disposition. Look at the famous hero of *Wuthering Heights*, Heathcliff. His physical characteristics described when introduced to readers accentuate his darkness; Nelly Dean even calls him an Oriental Prince. All this points to his being a misfit in the Earnshaw family and his later hero-villain-ish actions. We all loved that character and

saw a rationale behind his seemingly dark behavior, don't we?

2. **Social traits**- It covers culture, family, friends, career, and civil status; every element creates your social persona. Some of the social attributes also indicate the inner qualities of the character; For example, Mr. Knightley in Jane Austen's Emma owns his estate; he is single, related to the Woodhouse family, a mentor and mature friend to Emma, and an essential member of the Highbury social circle. the role he plays in Emma's growth and the friendship they share suggest a romantic development between the two as the narrative proceeds.

3. **Internal traits**- Inner attributes comprise the character's ethics, beliefs, attitudes, and experiences. These qualities dictate the character's choices based on which the narrative takes its turn. For example, the Sorting Hat puts Malfoy in Slytherin House because it could sense the ethical core of the character aligning with the values that House represented. But it placed Harry in Gryffindor because Harry chose to go there. The Hat saw a brilliant opportunity for Harry to succeed in Slytherin but respected his choice. Harry's moral core, beliefs, and attitude prompted him to choose Gryffindor over Slytherin.

4. **Psychological and emotional traits**- Besides internal character traits, the psychological and

emotional traits of the character are crucial. It comprises their mental health/stability, motivations, skills, strengths, weaknesses, and emotional intelligence. An unappreciated child will develop differently as an adult from a character with a secure childhood. When faced with a crisis, a character who could keep his nerve will take a different decision from the one who couldn't. Retaking the example of *Harry Potter*, Harry's worst fear was the dementors who played on his worst memories and incapacitated him to act. Eventually, he gathered his nerves and learned to use the defense charm 'Patronus' by conjuring up a happy memory. A lot depends on his emotional and psychological state and how he develops through the book (*Harry Potter and the Prisoner of Azkaban*).

These are the broad brush strokes to paint your characters. Now the question is how to lay these brushstrokes? It would help if you asked yourself some crucial questions to clarify your characters' attributes and motivations.

30 QUESTIONS TO CREATE A CHARACTER OUTLINE

Two major questions that should begin the probe into character outlining are: what do your characters look like, and what do they want besides the objective or desired 'goal'? In addition, here are some questions that the writers must ask to get to know their characters better:

- What does your character look like?
- Where do they come from? What is their ethnicity, culture, and ancestry?
- Do they have a personal style, some accessories, or preferred choice of clothes?
- Do they dress ordinarily or have a keen eye for fashion?
- Do they dress offensively, poorly, inappropriately, or provocatively as some other characters in the book?
- What hairstyles do they sport?
- Do they use styling products on their hair, go to the salon or do it on their own?
- What color is their hair? Is it their natural color, or do they like to sport quirky hair colors?
- How do they sport mustaches, beards, bushy eyebrows, or whiskers?
- Do they have clear skin or struggle with pimples?
- Are they of poor vision? If yes, then do they use contacts or wear specs?
- What kind of jewelry or watch do they wear? Are they fond of such accessories?
- Do they have a preferred variety of footwear?
- Are they fond of hats or any other headgear? What kind?

- Do they carry handbags? What sort of bags/purses do they usually take?
- Would they be okay with sporting a swimsuit in public?
- What kind of sleepwear do they prefer wearing during bedtime?
- What is remarkable about their persona? Do they ooze confidence or fidget in public?
- What is their characteristic body language?
- How do they stand? Do they stand tall or slouch?
- Do they have any peculiarities in movement, like a funny walk, or do they dance with two left feet? How do they run?
- Do they have a mark of identification like a scar or a birthmark?
- Do they have a tattoo? If yes, what's the significance or the memory saved in that tattoo? Does it have a story?
- Do they like any other form of body art, like piercing? If yes, what part of the body do they have pierced?
- Are any of your characters differently abled? If yes, then what kind of disability do they have?
- Are they quick-witted? Do they have good coordination? How soon or how well do they grasp things?
- Do they have a calm air, or are they clumsy and goofy?

- If anyone describes them in a few words, how would they see them – reasonably good-looking, ugly, mediocre-looking, ordinary or extraordinarily beautiful/handsome, cute, voluptuous, classy?
- If your book gets adapted into a movie, which actor would you like to cast in the role of that character?

The last question is the most complete as by the time you ask it and have an answer for it, you already have a clear vision of the character in your mind. Once you give them an outward shape in the actor you see playing them, your character ideation is complete.

Another exciting exercise in probing deeper into character development is to proceed with what-if questions. What if Harry Potter didn't have a scar on his face? What if Scout Finch had been a boy? What if Peter Pan finally grew up? What would he look like? Do this with the character you have just created. Checking alternative possibilities helps clarify whether you like the alternative or stick with the original plan. Whatever you choose, the final product should be something you are sure about.

HOW SHOULD CHARACTERS DEVELOP THROUGHOUT THE TIMELINE?

We have discussed that characters are primarily two types: round and flat. Flat characters remain the same throughout the story. Rounded characters go through a transformation from beginning to the end and hence are all the more interesting. Creating round characters speaks well for your novel's narrative as they keep the readers invested in the growth they undergo in the course of the story. Character development is integral and organic to plot development. The plot progresses as a character's journey through different life experiences – happy, sad, overwhelming, and overpowering – mostly life-changing. These experiences transform their character, lifestyle, perspective, and worldview. They take on a journey of self-discovery. They learn new lessons from their challenges, enabling them to achieve their goals. The best example of character development is seen in the *bildungsroman* or the novel of growth.

Examples include Joyce's *A Portrait of the Artist as a Young Man*, Jane Austen's *Emma*, Charlotte Bronte's *Jane Eyre*, and J.D. Salinger's *The Catcher in the Rye*. Let's take a closer look at how Emma's character develops through the plot of Austen's novel. Emma is a wealthy heiress, the daughter of Mr. Woodhouse, who remains unmarried to be with her father for the rest of his life. Though a good-intentioned woman with a noble heart, Emma lacks foresight and judgment and meddles in the love life of her friend and protege, Harriet, and other people in the Highbury society. Every time she makes a wrong judgment leading to her friend's heart getting broken, getting her embarrassed, or making her lose a good match, she learns a new lesson in life. Eventually, towards the end of the novel evolves into a wiser, maturer version of herself. Thanks to Mr. Knightley, who is always there as a conscience keeper of good sense. The influence of this character to a small extent and the learnings received from her failed attempts at 'fixing' other people's lives to a more significant extent lead to Emma's growth. Not only is she a changed woman, but she also finds love and life-long partnership in Mr. Knightley.

Each mistake, wrong judgment, failure, and correct decision takes your character one step closer to the person they become, the object/goal they seek, or the problem they are trying to solve. Character development happens in stages, and the first stage is to introduce your character to the readers. Introduce your main characters by name and early in things. Don't keep your reader waiting too long to meet the novel's protagonist or other main characters. Now naming is yet another art. You cannot resort to the technique of old parables where each character was named as an abstract quality they stand for. However, it would be best to keep their names consonant with their ethnic identity; The title should reflect their heritage and perhaps hint at their personality.

The next step is to lead your reader to visualize that character. Do not impose how you see them on your reader; there will be physical and character trait descriptions, but don't go for over-detailing. Leave room for your reader to decide if their Sherlock is Robert Downey Junior or Benedict Cumberbatch. Once visualized, make your character more real by giving them a history, a backstory. Character history is all that happened before the narrative of your book started. But do not spell out the past in one go because it's like sharing one's entire life's story on the first date! Details like family background, cultural heritage, profession, relationship status, skills and talents, faith, and politics are the components of a backstory.

In the next step, you must humanize your main characters. Give them flaws and vulnerabilities. Remember, Bruce Wayne could transform into Batman only by transforming his fear of bats into his symbol. Peter Parker was bullied at school, and hence he is more relatable. So when he becomes Spiderman, he remains relatable to the average youngster. Classic potentialities balance these vulnerabilities to become remarkable characters. Otherwise, why would you write their story? Well-developed characters must do extraordinary things and yet stay relatable to the masses. Every superhero we know becomes one out of one desire – to help people and make the world a better place. This goes beyond the other distinctive super heroic features like the ability to fly or jump from building to building. A classic example of the vulnerabilities of a hero without making him cowardly is seen in George Bernard Shaw's portrayal of Captain Bluntschli in *Arms and the Man*. He is a sleep-deprived mercenary soldier who fled the battlefield and threatened to kill Raina if she revealed to the search party he was hiding in her room. He is hungry, sleepy, and nervous, but that doesn't make him a coward when we know the horrible experiences and realities of war he had witnessed in the last couple of days. We understand Bluntschli as a practical soldier who values food over arsenal and staying alive over sacrificing his life foolishly on the battlefield to prove a point. He is vulnerable yet heroic in the true sense.

In the next stage, probe a little deeper into the hero's mind. What keeps them awake at night, their fears and ambitions, what embarrasses or upsets them, and what makes them genuinely happy. Talk to people around you or draw upon your own experiences. The best part of writing a novel is the opportunity of living many lives, so make the best out of it. Lived experiences help develop your characters at a more authentic level. Try to think like that character; instead, become that character. Another golden rule of character development, as we have discussed in plot development, is to show more and tell less. You are not giving your reader enough credit to figure their way out through the character's journey by telling everything. But the reading experience will be more engaging and satisfying if you lead them on to figure out details. So let your character reveal themselves through their body language, thoughts, attitudes, and actions.

Last and the essential condition for character development is to conduct thorough research. Avoid writing something you haven't had a first-hand experience with without conducting in depth research. Suppose your character is a professional mountaineer, and you have never even made a short trekking trip. There, it's better to interview people from that profession, read about mountaineering, and keep researching until you are confident about looking at your novel's world from the eyes of that professional mountaineer. The biggest challenge comes in writers writing about a different gender. Imagine the challenge of a male writer writing about a female lead who had just had a miscarriage. They must observe and interact with their female friends and relatives to understand the lived experience of a woman's life for emotional knowledge and read up on medical writings to understand the bodily impact. Thorough research is the key to getting yourself in the skin of a character so different from you.

CHARACTER OUTLINE TEMPLATE

Having a ready-to-use template for writers is another idea to add value to the book. So if you must create one, make it into a form or template like you fill up for creating a CV or a portfolio. It should incorporate these items for better detailing:

- The character's name, age, sex, and date of birth for the convenience of time-lining
- Family details (family and family background, like parents, siblings, extended family, etc.)
- Hometown and residence
- Relationship status
- Friendship circle

- Social circle and acquaintances
- Their relationship with men and women
- Profession and relationship with colleagues
- Appearance and personal style (show how they dress and accessorize)
- Faith and beliefs
- Attitude to religion and spirituality
- Politics
- Worldview/philosophy of life
- Interests and hobbies (sports, travel, reading, arts, investments)
- Eating and drinking habits
- The goal in life/ambition
- Most vital positive and negative traits
- Other traits that must be developed through the story
- Attitude to people in general (considerate or indifferent, kind or insensitive)
- People's perception of the character
- The character's perception of themselves
- Most remarkable trait about this character
- Whether the reader will like or dislike the character and why?

Create a one to two-page document with these items briefly described in one or two sentences. You can choose a tabular form for better readability and organization.

Planning your character is the most significant milestone to cover before you write. You have your plot outlined, but if the people who populate the story and translate it into action are not visualized, writing cannot have a proper direction. Now that you are familiar with your characters, the next step, to break your content into chapters. If you follow my instructions, this should be a cakewalk.

6

BREAKING DOWN THE BRILLIANCE INTO CHAPTERS

So far, you have a plot outline, a character outline template, umpteen Post-its, flashcards, and sticky notes to get yourself started. But none of this will have a definite structure if you don't organize your material in a chapter-wise break-up. A chapter-by-chapter outline brings the ideas together and helps structure a novel, ensuring enough time and information is in each core part of the book. Let's see how you divide your material in a decent chapter-wise flow. You get to see all your formulae and theories put into plot outlining and chunking the total material into a rough beginning, middle, and end, coming into a practical chaptered form.

WHAT SHOULD EACH CHAPTER CONTAIN

The rule of thumb is to imagine each chapter as a milestone. That takes the reader closer to the end goal, the novel's denouement. Looking at chapters in this light helps visualize them as one complete unit contributing to the novel's overall structure. So each chapter has to have a purpose that organically relates to the bigger picture. Keeping a few points in mind will make your work much more manageable.

- Start with action to interest the reader. A character navigating the traffic on a busy Monday morning will incite more reader interest than one musing over a cup of coffee in the opening scene. There are exceptions when the second type can work just as acceptable or even better, but as a general rule, try to begin your first chapter in the middle of things. The Romans call it 'medias res,' starting in the middle of the action.
- Develop the plot with a crucial piece of information. It can be an unresolved conflict, a foreboding, a looming question, a character's internal conflict, or anything that makes the reader ask, 'what next.' To heighten readers' interest and keep them craving more, writers often prefer ending each chapter with a hook or a cliffhanger.
- Have a specific goal for each chapter, be clear on the key takeaway from each chapter. Suppose you create

a chapter revolving around the senior year prom night; the significant takeaways from this can be introducing the reader to the main characters and informing them about their dynamics. Some chapters can be devoted to exploring the character's inner life, some introduce new characters, and others are highly action or altercation oriented. Identify the need each chapter serves and stick to that scheme throughout that chapter.

- Chapters help keep track of the pacing of your narrative. For instance, slightly longish chapters are meant for flashbacks, presenting a character's back story, or some rumination and introspection. Shorter chapters are more action/reaction-oriented quick page-turners. Some chapters give your readers more food for thought; they pause, read and reread to capture the essence. Others are for the reader to rush through. Besides the reading pace, Having chapters also regulates the narrative rate, as some chapters allow the characters to pause and ruminate on what just happened. Others involve action, reaction, and quick thinking.
- Include different characters' points of view; there can either be competing character points of view or shifting POVs in each chapter. You get to incorporate the thoughts and attitudes of different characters by including different narrative perspectives and voices in separate chapters. You get buy-ins from other

characters, which makes it an engaging read. Also, your narrative is balanced and not one-sided.
- Find a balance between scene and dramatic narration in your chapters. A scene captures the action and what happens in the course of the narrative. Dramatic narration reports what occurs outside the narrative. Try to find a balance between two modes of writing in your chapters – too much dramatic narration can be monotonous, and too many action-oriented scenes can be an overkill for the reader. A simple hack is to highlight the scenes and leave the dramatic narration parts unhighlighted. This will give you a bird's eye view of the entire thing; you will know where to add and what to subtract to strike the balance.

Chapter-outlining gives a clear view of how your novel will shape up, but do not worry too much about clear chapter breaks in the first draft. There will be rounds of revision where you can fix it. While outlining, you need a rough sketch to keep going at it. Another technique is to come up with some provisional chapter titles. These may not be definitive but give you a distilled focus on where your story comes from and where it's headed next. But don't get too attached to these titles, as a more exciting and relevant title may come up during the writing process.

HOW TO END A CHAPTER

There are different ways to end a chapter. Most chapters will end with a cliffhanger, so the reader is compelled to start the next chapter. There are different ways this technique can be employed, like asking a question, revealing character development, or offering some wisdom.

One way to do it is by asking a question. Ending the chapter with a question leaves the reader waiting rather than searching for an answer. Let's take an example from Adam Johnson's *The Orphan Master's Son*:

> *"But where are [the answers]?" Jun Do asked. He could see the girl rower shooting flares his way, and he could feel the Mate's cold cheek as the sharks pulled him under. "Will we ever find them?"*
>
> Jun Do has recently lied that his Second Mate died in a shark attack instead of being defected in North Korea. The interrogator knows he is lying and doesn't even care. Jun Do feels despair, feels guilty, and wants something to be true. The question which the author leaves the readers at the end of the chapter reinforces the central theme – there is no truth, only contesting stories, and the best version wins.

There are several other ways of ending a chapter. You can create a sense of foreboding by introducing a character – leave the readers in anticipation of the character's motives, actions, and intent and how it will affect the lives of your main characters with whom the reader has formed a kinship. In this technique, you do not ask a question but plant anticipation in the reader's mind. Various textual strategies include introducing a new character, an unexpected turn of events, or a character caught in a moral dilemma. This makes the readers frame their questions and look forward to the answers.

Another exciting and rather graceful use of the cliffhanger technique is to end your chapter in some wisdom or a metaphor. This example from Michael Chabon's *Amazing Adventures of Kavalier and Clay* should clarify it:

> "The true magic of this broken world lay in the ability of the things it contained to vanish, to become so thoroughly lost, that they might never have existed in the first place."

In a book about magic, how profound it is for the characters to claim they have recognized the true nature of magic.

Another instance of such a highly philosophical and wise ending is found in the last chapter of E.M. Forster's *A Passage to India*, but since that's the final chapter, let's save it for another discussion… And here I ended this segment with a cliffhanger:)

SHOULD CHAPTERS BE NAMED?

Chapters can set the scene, create anticipation or suspense, or even just a sneak peek of what is to come. But whether to title them or not is purely a personal artistic preference. There might be some title ideas for the outline stage, but most would agree that chapter titles can be decided on after the first draft. However, I am not discouraging you from keeping a record of the possible titles as they give a direction and contribute to the style and voice of each chapter. It helps organize and keep track of which chapter covers what by the title. The naming convention has its upside, but do not force it in the outlining phase. Keep things flexible and provisional so you can turn them around during the first draft revision.

Chapter titles add an element of foreshadowing and heighten the reader's interest, but if they do not come out as striking or significant value additions to your work later (writing and revision stage), feel free not to use them at all!

IS THERE AN IDEAL LENGTH FOR A CHAPTER?

There are no rules on chapter length, only guidelines. For instance, looking at the 18th century novel *Tristram Shandy* by Laurence Sterne, you will realize how unconventional chapter lengths or formation can be a potent artistic tool. The book was written much ahead of its time technique-wise, as we find the writer using black and blank pages in some chapters. Wonder what that does to the chapter word count? Isn't the artistic principle behind creating such chapters beyond word count-bound chapterization?

However, if you are a new writer who needs a ballpark target, I will give you a fair estimate. Most chapters are between 1,500 and 5,000, the sweet spot being between 3,000 and 4,000. However, Jodi Picoult's latest novel had a highly unusual chapter setup that worked well with the plot. Chapter 7 was one word, 8, 9, and 10 were 2 or 3 sentences, and chapter 11 was less than two pages.

Remember, I already discussed the average word count for an adult fiction novel is between 80,000 and 100,000 words. 25% should be the beginning, 50% the middle, and 25% the end. This ratio will help plan some of the chapter lengths. Chapter breaks are essential as they offer the material in digestible chunks to process and mull over. It also prepares the reader for a change in narrative POV, incident, or shift. The reader might have a bumpy ride if the chapters are too short. Too short chapters do not allow you to build up the momentum and the acclimatization time the reader needs to go along with the story.

The tech-savvy reader of this digital era has a lower attention span than the readers of yesteryears. They prefer reading blogs over research articles for necessary information. But if a chapter is too long, it risks losing the reader forever. It would be best if you were sensitive to how long you, as a reader, would like to linger on one chapter to decide when to stop and when to stretch one chapter.

However, all things said and done, it is an artistic decision, so do not feel curbed by any hard and fast rules of chapter length. Just remember you can read for hours if its interesting but you will struggle to read for seconds if its not.

I am discussing the outlining phase here so the ballparks mentioned above can act as some milestone or an organizing principle. When you start the writing process of the first draft, you cannot bind yourself too much to these numbers. Let it out on paper, and the word count audit can be performed more closely during the editing and revision rounds.

Getting carried away with chapters in an outline can always come in the way of your creativity. Restrict yourself to using chapters in your design only to weave the characters, settings, timeline, and plot together. Generally, a chapter break will take the reader back or encourage them to look forward. So it is better to decide when and where to start and finish a chapter after the first draft.

OUTLINE ADVICE FOR CHILDREN'S BOOKS

Do you believe that children's literature is only meant for children? Well, guess what? Most children's literature is equally appealing to adults. So many of my friends read *Harry Potter* for the first time in their thirties and were glued to it from books one to seven. However, for outlining a children's book, you must be mindful of the target demographic. Think like a child

– what inspires a child, holds them in awe, makes them happy or sad, and how they perceive the adult world in a gleeful sense of wonder. Explore that natural state of joy and the innate sense of wonder at everything that's part and parcel of childhood, and you have your climate for a storyline.

EXTRA CONSIDERATIONS FOR A CHILDREN'S BOOK OUTLINE

Don't think that just because the average age of the reader is younger, it would simplify the process; on the contrary, it makes things rather tricky. To an extent, the structure remains the same as adult fiction, with the four main core components: plot, setting, timeline, and character. The story arrangement also follows the same progression milestones: a beginning, a middle, and an end riven with plot points and twists and turns to the denouement or conclusion.

However, there are two main distinguishing features you need to focus on while outlining a children's book: the attention span of the reader and a moral takeaway. A child's attention span is much shorter than an adult's. Adults can get lost in a book, but children can't hold their attention for that long. Typically, a child's attention span is two or three times their age. A five-year-old will have a maximum attention span of 15 minutes. Hence try to keep your story free from too many distractions or digressions. This includes subplots, backstories, and too many character tracks. Instead, streamline your plot around the main storyline, which should have some symbolic significance. An allegorical medium often works wonders for children's literature; Use allegory as an extended metaphor. The best example is *Gulliver's Travels*. The allegorical fabric is so solid and multi-layered in this book it does not remain confined to the label of a children's book. Remember, children's literature is mainly targeted at the child reader but not confined to them. The readership goes beyond the primary target demographic.

How often did I read and wonder at *Aesop's Fables* as a child? The main reason allegory can be an interesting tool in children's writing brings us to the second distinguishing feature – the moral teaching or takeaway. As we see in most fables, allegory can be a decent technique to incorporate the moral education disguised under an entertaining story.

So the basic structure is streamlined into four components: the beginning, middle, climax, and end. There should be no meandering between acts; not too many internal monologues or introspective scenes should be incorporated. Coming to characterization, don't be shy of exciting and fun new characters to interact with your main character. We fondly remember The Mad Hatter from *Alice in Wonderland* and Baloo and Bagheera from *The Jungle Book*. Another crucial point you must pay special attention to is your story's build-up or the climax. This is where the complication reaches its height, the moment just before the resolution follows – a monster is about to be slain or a treasure to be found. Make sure that your climax is a very clear-cut resolution of the complication introduced initially and developed through the middle of the story. The way your characters handle the climax determines the highest point of their growth or development throughout the book. The climax inadvertently leads to the end, where all the missing pieces come together, and your reader should be left with some moral or wisdom. So devising a wholesome conclusion is significant to successfully outlining children's books.

HOW DOES JULIA DONALDSON OUTLINE HER BOOKS?

Julia Donaldson, an English writer and playwright, has some interesting book outlining methods. She has 184 published works, sold over 5 million copies, and her books have been translated into 81 languages. For Donaldson, the source of inspiration can be anywhere: her childhood memories, things happening in her children's lives, the places she visits, the old folktales and fairy tales, and so on. Getting an idea is not really the hard part; the challenge comes with organizing it into a beginning, a middle, and an end. Naturally, it takes months, even years, for her to let that idea grow and plan a book. She starts the actual writing process only when she is ready, which takes anything from a week with picture books, to six months to write a chapter book. For instance, Donaldson took one year to plan the Gruffalo and just one week to write it. This is evidence enough to the premise that planning is the more complicated part than the actual writing process; once your planning is fool-proof, the rest is relatively smooth sailing.

Her writing process is as enjoyable as ideation. Donaldson uses a pencil or pen and a large notebook for rhyming stories. She keeps doodling along the way. She prefers using the computer to write a story that doesn't rhyme.

ROALD DAHL'S WRITING TECHNIQUE

"Those who don't believe in magic will never find it."

This profound quote from Roald Dahl has as broad an audience as his works, and it rings true for his writing and thought process too. That's why the settings of his stories are primarily modern-day fairy tale worlds to appeal to a child's imagination. His writing style involves a lot of good humor characteristic to the interest level of his target demographic – children often love reading funny stories with characters behaving in an absurd manner, using nonsense words. Lewis Carrol used this technique of nonsense words and fantastical/magical settings in the classic children's book *Alice in Wonderland*. The tradition has been carried on by the children's writers of the posterity in their signature style.

In Dahl's fictional world, we meet many characters with interesting names; he makes sure that his nomenclature appropriately defines the characters and helps the reader identify them. Not just do his silly character names betray their personality traits. Still, Dahl's overuse of descriptive adjectives provides the reader with a lot of information about the characters and their situation. This makes for an easy reading experience and keeps the reader hooked without making too much effort. The reader's interest grows spontaneously. A cherry on top is his signature use of language. He twists and invents new words and experiments with sentence structure for an immersive reading experience. His language use is poetic, with a generous sprinkling of metaphors, similes, alliteration, and puns. Also, we must not forget his penchant for inventing onomatopoeias, words that represent abstract sounds.

Personification plays a significant role in Dahl's stories. He often transforms characters, especially animals, into a human form and vice versa, giving them a mind of their own; he makes them think and speak like humans. Dahl's world is populated by all sorts; there's a perfect balance of the good and the bad, the nice and the nasty, which keeps the reader grounded in reality. He never presents a world too good to be true. His portrayal of child characters is fascinating; he often portrays them better than adults, giving the child reader a taste of how a child's imagination works in a world like this.

THE INCREDIBLE MIND OF DR. SEUSS

To further understand the value of outlining, let's look into the incredible story of Dr. Seuss's posthumous publication *What Pet Should I Get*. After Theodor Seuss Geisel died in 1991, his wife Audrey found a box of unseen creations that showed us how Dr. Seuss took his ideas and turned them into children's works of art. The famous American children's author was not just an illustrator and cartoonist; he was a poet and filmmaker. Audrey then donated the illustrations and early drafts to the University of California and stocked some sketches and doodles in a box. Much later in 2013, when the remaining contents in the box were closely examined, it turned out to be a treasure trove. Some rough sketches were titled "The Horse Museum," a brightly colored set of alphabet flashcards, and a folder marked "Noble failures." But besides all this, there was a much more complete set of work, a project labeled "The Pet Shop." It was a story with 16 black and white illustrations and typed text taped next to them. If Dr. Seuss had not had this outlining strategy in place, the world would be deprived of the posthumous title *What Pet Should I Get*. That's the significance and power of outlining – you can dig treasure out of a box of unused scrap art material and turn it into a full-length book title.

POINTS TO REMEMBER

Remember that from fantasy to mystery to comedy, children love reading most of the popular literary genres that adult readers find fascinating. The most significant point of departure is your major characters' perspectives and thought processes throughout the narrative. So, when planning a children's book, one of the most important things to remember is that the outline should contain a lot of information from the child's viewpoint. How would the child react to the plot or a character, or how would a child imagine a setting description. To think like a kid, you can fall back on your childhood memories – your aspirations, hopes, desires, fears, failures, successes, friendships, and new experiences; everything can be your food for thought. This helps establish empathy with your target audience's mindset. Another way is to interact with and observe children. Spend time understanding the kids around you, your own or your friends' or families. A child always has a different perspective from adults because their mind's eye is not burdened by too many happy/sad experiences that come with the adult years. The trick is to retain that freshness of perspective. Kids seem to live in the moment and don't, on the whole, have troubles on their minds. They are usually not used to disappointments and constantly expect the best to happen, so your story must consider this to get the best balance. It differs from writing for adults but no less skilled, and your account can be as good as any book written solely for a mature audience.

Another vital strategy is to know what's selling in the market. This might sound less artistic and more on the business side of writing, but it's all part of the game. Know what appeals to the kid of this day? Is it a Peter Pan, a Harry Potter, or perhaps a Percy Jackson? Would you know the answer if asked that question? Besides characterization, perform a genre-wise survey to determine your audience's taste – what are they reading, fantasy or sci-fi, magic or mystery? Knowing what grabs the children's interest is essential before you outline your novel because one thing you must always be mindful of is the dwindling attention span of a child reader. Consider the Amazon top 100 children's books, and that will give you at least a snippet of what is popular at the moment; it may show you a gap in the market, or it may show you a trend that's exciting to jump on board with. If you're serious about selling books, don't go into this without knowing your audience.

This brings us to another vital part of your homework – read a lot of children's literature, both contemporary bestsellers and classics. It will help you understand the child reader's taste and how to create and stick to the child's perspective in writing your book. You also get to learn a lot of literary hacks to make your book an engaging read. Simple themes, unsophisticated sentence structure, nonsense words, and fun characters are a few literary elements that can always be found in the bestselling works or in the classics by the masters of children's literature.

The rule of thumb for the art of characterization of any form of literature, be it children's or adult fiction, is to have a character in whom your readers see a reflection of themselves. For example, Ron Weasley is a relatable regular boy at school who would pay less attention to the lessons and won't score straight A's in every subject. He is not as extraordinary a wizard as Harry or a genius like Hermione, yet he has a heroic quality and is loyal -- he is the greatest friend a kid can have in their coming of age years. All these human qualities in a wizard bring him close to the reader, perhaps closer than Harry at times! In my search to improve my writing and find great fiction from all over the world. I read stories from all corners of the globe to see if different cultures still have the same values and needs as my own. I discovered another exemplary child character called *Swami* from R.K.

Narayan's *Swami and Friends, an Indian book trilogy*. Swami, from his bid to impress the new boy in class to his desire to possess a simple bicycle wheel. His faking of fever to bunk off school and his curiosity and innocent envy towards his newborn baby brother showed me that kids seem to have the same basic feelings no matter where they are from. Swami is a regular second grader growing up in a 1930s middle-class Indian family, but the story could just as easily have been about a kid growing up in Britain in the 1930s or even today. His ordinary hopes and disappointments make him likable to the typical child or adult reader. It also showed me that the way kids think is universal; they require things so common and basic that most of us forgot years ago that we had felt the same way once. I recall as a seven year-old wanting a tiny crystal that another classmate owned so much I tried to put it in my pocket and walk away with it, but I didn't get far. I was embarrassed to get caught with it. Still, that little fragment of crystal, the size of a penny was so shiny and unique that it made me want it so much. Today I walk past better examples of crystals on the ground and don't bat an eyelid; they don't impress adults because we have seen them often for years. We must remember children are playful, often mischievous, and sometimes jealous over small things. So when writing about a child's character, we must show these things, and importantly they must have a growth trajectory throughout the narrative. They are growing and learning, which is a journey; they must have emotional arcs and some wisdom to arrive at or some goal to be accomplished by the end of the story. This makes for a rewarding reading experience for the child reader.

To conclude, think like a child (perspective), feel like a child (emotional arcs), and act like a child (characterization) in your book to create a perfect outline for children's fiction.

8

OUTLINE ADVICE FOR ROMANCE NOVELS

From *Anna Karenina* to *Pride and Prejudice,* from *Gone with the Wind* to *The Fault in Our Stars,* romance novels are among the most popular genres amongst readers. And there's ample evidence to support this claim. U.K.'s leading romance novel publishers, Mills & Boons, publishes 720 titles a year, a number they wouldn't have touched, let alone consistently maintained, had there been any less demand in the reading community. So what does the average reader look for when they pick up a romance novel? From the sophisticated to the sinful, the overflow of powerful emotions to the flux of passion, each romance novel has one thing in common: an instant catapult into an exciting world of new love and lust. After reading the Twilight Saga, my niece considered marrying a vampire very seriously. Sadly for her, she's not met any to date.

Instant escape also means instant gratification for the reader. Hence a rewarding reading experience, a lot of dopamine rushes, and a feel-good factor at the prospect of a 'happily ever after' are the driving factors behind the success of this genre. So, if you are just starting your journey to outline your first book, romance seems like an excellent way to go, as the chances of being sold are pretty high. And I mean serious business here; doing a fabulous job with your romance novel can make you commercially successful in many ways. The demand for romance novels being turned into movies is relatively high for the same obvious reason of escape and instant gratification. So, let's take a deep dive into the pool of ideas and methods that go into outlining a novel in the romance genre.

WHAT DOES A ROMANCE NOVEL NEED?

So you have a basic idea in your mind, some rough character sketches, and even visualize a few scenes like how your characters meet for the first time, or when they have a moment of epiphany about their feelings for each other, what next? The next step is to create the outline, and while doing so, you must keep all other essentials of a romance novel in mind. Some certain tropes or conventions are the core ingredients of a good romance novel. For starters, you must have a three-act structure as an organizing principle comprising the setup, complication/confrontation, and resolution. Then in each stage of your plot development, you must incorporate specific elements. Don't worry; you can still have a unique story with this structure. Let's discuss each stage one by one:

- **The unique meet:** So, how does the boy meet the girl? The best kick-off for your romance novel is how your main characters, destined to fall in love, meet? In script writing, it's called the 'meet-cute'. There can be a million ways in which your two characters meet. They can meet anywhere and anyhow – they can be living in buildings opposite each other's, run into each other in a library, become lab partners on the first day of high school, or one saves the other from an accident. On a scale of ordinary to extraordinary, you can design your meet-cute as anything that creates anticipation in the reader's mind about this first meeting being pregnant with possibilities of many happy developments, though the attraction is not instant. Take the example of *Pride and Prejudice*. Elizabeth meets Mr. Darcy for the first time in a ball, where he makes some demeaning comments about her within her earshot. This first meeting doesn't seem to be a pleasant start but holds the reader anticipating developments in due course. Suppose your characters already know each other, let's say they are childhood buddies or neighbors. Still, an extraordinary meeting is significant as this is how the readers see them together on the pages connecting for the first time. The more unique the meet, the more excited your reader gets to follow through the story. For example, in the movie Spiderman with Toby Maguire, he lives next door to his future girlfriend, but she never really notices him until he defeats the school bully after receiving his new powers. That is where her blinkers are suddenly removed.

- **The main character's dilemma:** Now that the main characters have met, you must create some build-up for the readers' engagement. Keep your characters debating the next step: should they call them, should they confront them if the first meeting didn't go well, should they do a little background search, or should they write to them? Take the reader through the mindscape of your characters. This usually is through dialog with a secondary character in a book. They want to get in touch and grow a relationship, but something is in the way. Even if it is a love-at-first-sight setting, love should never come easy to your characters. Remember, nothing worth having comes easy. The goals are worthy only if the stakes are high or the road is difficult. In romance novels, sometimes it's either an external complication or your characters' innate nature that might come in the way of a successful love story. It can be an internal or external obstacle. For example, the object of their desires is an old friend's ex, and he could lose a friend, or perhaps her family is in a different class of society and would look down on the pursuer. Identify that complication for your characters and set them on a journey to overcome it and find love at the end.

- **The main character's choice:** After the difficulties and challenges are identified, the onus is on your main characters to make grave choices. Your protagonist is torn between the emotional states created by the meet-cute and the cons involved in following their heart. Think of Edward from the *Twilight* saga; a part of him cannot stay away from Bella; he wants to fight it because he might be aroused by her scent and crave her blood or bring her to harm. The vampire-human predicament is the complication in Edward's life (before other complications appear). Ultimately, he has to choose -- the choice of being with Bella to keep her safe.
- **The tropes:** At this point in your romance novel outline, your characters would be seeing a lot more of each other, so you would like to consider some tropes. It can be anything like the lovers-to-rivals trope where they enter a contest against the love

interest. For example, they both run for class president, or the friends-to-lovers trope where they take up a job, a class, or a place in proximity with the love interest to get a chance to get to know each other as friends first. These tropes often act as the inciting action, the first plot point after which there's no turning back for the characters.

- **Romantic tension:** The first plot point inadvertently leads to romantic tension. Now the characters are getting to know each other better, trust each other more, and things are getting serious. This is a point where you give the readers what they came expecting in the rising action – the conflict. As the characters grow more fond of each other, they must have some strong reason not to fully commit. There can be external factors like a clan rivalry between their families, a third person, a competitor, a career move that requires relocation, an ideological difference between the characters, or some misunderstanding that should make the success of the love story seem like an impossibility. Brew your conflict so it doesn't seem like a forced non-issue; it should be organic to the situation, the other characters' conflicting motives, and the nature of the main characters themselves. All the challenges keeping Darcy falling for Elizabeth and vice versa are the outcome of his prejudice and her pride.

- **A shakeup:** You are at the midpoint of your story outline now, where you create an illusion of happiness in the characters' future. It's a point where they confess their feelings to each other, kiss, or indicate that they have fallen for each other. Still, they are jumping the gun because now you must design some turn of events that suggests that their happily ever after is just around the corner and then snatch it from them. It's eventually a false defeat, but you want to convince the reader for the time being that they can't be together after all by creating some crisis. The return of an old love interest or some situation that makes them question their feelings for each other. You don't resolve the conflict but let it brew until the final showdown – the climax and the denouement.
- **The lesson:** When you are approximately 75% of the narrative, let your characters find a way back to each other in learning a lesson. It can be an introspection or experiential learning that brings an epiphany to the character about their true feelings, why they had been in denial, or why they were holding back. They realize the value of their feelings and acknowledge that if they want a happily ever after, they must overcome whatever is blocking their way back to the love interest. This should map to the conflict brewing throughout the narrative, external or internal. For example, Edward fighting the Volturi in

Twilight Saga or Elizabeth and Darcy confronting their own mental blocks and seeing each other's true nature in an unbiased light, this is where your characters must have a moment of clarity. The story reaches the second plot point here.

- **Falling in Love:** This is the point of total transparency as the characters lay bare their hearts to each other when they are the most vulnerable and the strongest at the same time because the feelings are acknowledged and reciprocated.
- **The split:** now their hearts are on their sleeves; the conflict returns with a vengeance and makes the final blow; this sets the characters apart again. This move will ensure they become reunited with more ferocity in the end.
- **The rebuilding:** The characters now salvage the broken pieces of their relationship and start rebuilding it. This is the climactic moment where they must pay a considerable price for staying together. For instance, if the conflict is due to disapproving parents, they must stand up to them; if it's a job offer from far away, they muster the courage to turn it down for love. This is the final commitment with no going back; they burn bridges and show no regrets.
- **A glimpse into the happily ever after:** Now that the final conflict has been sorted out, we are one step closer to their forever of happiness. Give your

readers a slice of the happy denouement so the whole read seems worth it. This is actually a skinny slice; set up the happiness and let the readers imagine what joys they have to come. It's the cherry on the cake, the satisfying conclusion everyone wants.

In romance novels, many elements from the above list develop differently given the character/s whose life you are writing about. Their choices and traits decide significant plot twists and inner conflicts, which are the thoroughfare of romance. When you incorporate all the core elements above into your plot outline's three-act design, keep your character arcs developing simultaneously.

WHAT CAN WE TAKE FROM THE AUTHOR OF THE NOTEBOOK

At the moment of writing, Nicholas Sparks has written 17 novels, 9 of which have been turned into movies. His advice to fellow writers is to read a lot of books. Reading a lot is integral to your research and skill development. By a lot of books, Sparks means like a hundred books a year; well, he has been doing the same since he was 15. I doubt many of us have the time to do that. Read many books in different genres penned by various authors as every book adds something new to your knowledge base. Some will teach you how to create suspense around the characters' motivations, some will teach you how to give quirks or humorous attributes to the characters, and some will teach you the art of staying inside the character's head in an internal monologue. The more varied your reading list, the more varied your learnings of the mechanics of writing will be. The secret is to stop when enjoying a paragraph and say to yourself, what was it about this paragraph that made me love it. It will disrupt the reading flow, but it will teach you the tricks that great authors use.

The next step is to ask many questions about those books: where were the plot surprises? When does the reader meet the good/bad guy? What was the impact of that meeting? So, if you are outlining a romance novel, you can ask questions like how the main characters were made to meet? Was it unique enough? How does the complication make its way into the story? Were the characters' dilemmas forced or in keeping with their personality traits? The more questions you ask, the more information you have for your outline.

The last and the most crucial step, according to Sparks, is to simply write. Did you know that the author of *The Notebook* wrote two complete novels and a non-fiction book before he wrote *The Notebook* and had it published? Those first books never got published, but they taught Sparks two things: he could write and finish a book if he became dedicated to the art. Serious writing comes only when you know you can pull up the craft, roll up your sleeves, and actually get working. So if a new writer embarks on writing as a serious profession, they must make it a habit to write regularly. Sparks himself writes five to six times every week, at least 2000 words or more. Consistency is the key.

SIMPLICITY AND COMPLEXITY OF JANE AUSTEN

Jane Austin's books were written simple, but it was a deceptively simple style as the plots and characters were complex. First, the characters weren't limited to a few. There were often details about the members of each family and the relationships between the different classes. She won't pick one or two main characters and develop them, but entire families, acquaintances, family friends, and the entire social circle of these families; within her range, she made her characterization as elaborate and complex as possible. This resulted from knowing her world exceptionally well.

Austen's oeuvre is a classic example of making the best out of the limited world you know in English literature. Her setting is the provincial 19th century England, rich in its beauty, but the natural scenery is hardly her area of focus. Instead, her subject was the study of Man as a social being, human nature per se, and the whole nexus of a human's social existence, which contributes to the complexity of her plots. The setting and characters are based on all real actual people and places she had lived in and around. Her characters are mainly the landed gentry, the upper class, the lower clergy, lower nobility, and the military corps, the kind she knew and interacted with intimately. The industrial and agrarian masses, working class and lower class, are absent from her character gallery.

The main characters followed the plot, but there were often numerous subplots with other characters. Let's take the example of *Emma*. The main story revolves around the Emma Knightley relationship and Emma's development as an individual. The subplot has many strings – we have Harriett Smith's love life, Mr. Elton and Frank Churchill, who are intricately involved in Emma's social life as possible suitors. It's worth noting that Austen didn't only focus on character development but also on intellectual and moral development. The story of Emma has a simultaneous inward and outward movement. The inward is all about what Emma thinks is happening, and the outer involves what is actually happening. The contrast between the two brings to light Emma's mistakes, her errors of judgment, and self-deception which leads to embarrassments and self-reproach, ultimately leading her to the path of self awareness. The intellectual and moral development shown by all her main characters in different novels makes Austen one of the foremost practitioners of the bildungsroman, a sort of coming-of-age novel set in 18th-century literature.

Whether it's an 18th-century classic exploring social positions and marriage or a modern, steamy sequel, a romantic novel outline should have one main goal that is the key to success. The key is to take the reader away from the stress and anxiety of today's world and let them escape into a troublesome but fun situation that will have a happy ending. Yes, happy resolution, or as we call it, 'happily ever after,' is the carrot dangling for your reader. If morbidity and tragedy were what they were looking for, they would have picked up another genre, like the dystopian novel or war fiction. So make sure while you write an outline for a romance novel, you have a clear notion of how you resolve the complications so everything falls in place in your characters' world.

OUTLINE FOR THRILLER AND HORROR NOVELS

Believe it or not, the readers love to sit on the edge of their seats, biting their nails, and savor the chill running down their spine. Yes, I am talking about the never-ending craving for the thriller and horror genre among the reading community. The writers are aware of this preference, and that's why the space is already saturated. So to make your work in this genre remarkable, the challenge is creating fresh ideas that don't just recycle a previous novel. This challenge is where an outline will give the writer an advantage. It gives them an organizing principle for their creativity and an opportunity to compare notes. That is, if in the outline you see your protagonist marooned in a hotel unoccupied by guests with his family, his psychological degeneration escalating into chasing his wife and child with an ax, you know you are at risk of regurgitating *The Shining*. This easy error may make you rethink your setting or approach a different build-up for the climax.

BE SPECIFIC ABOUT THE SUBGENRE

There are umpteen subgenres within thriller and horror fiction. Thrillers are full of tension and unexpected plot twists; every chapter and almost every scene is a cliffhanger. There are at least eight types of thriller subgenres: psychological, action, political, legal, science fiction, spy, crime, or mystery. Therefore, it is vital to identify the subgenre before getting started to give your vision more focus.

The same goes for the horror genre. The subgenres include demonic possession, witchcraft, paranormal activity, monster, vampire, psychological, zombie, serial killers, gore, and even comedic horror. Identifying the genre helps you decide how you treat the horror element early on. For instance, psychological horror is more like a Coleridgean poem about an implied horror than a ghost floating around the living room while you are supping quietly in the kitchen. It's more about feeling something is there than it being there. Zombie horror, on the contrary, will give the horror element a material physical form. Likewise, the gory and slasher or serial killer genres inspire fear through cringing bloodshed and horrific incidents. The comedy-horror brings a non-scary, often gory, and feel-good element into the supernatural (we all love *Shaun of the Dead*, don't we?).

Thriller and horror genre thrives on how it affects the readers, and these finer subgeneric distinctions are integral to deciding how your plot shall proceed through the twist and turns, suspense, and build-up.

5 ELEMENTS TO INCLUDE IN YOUR THRILLER/HORROR OUTLINE

Every thriller/horror fiction outline has one necessity – there should be no plot holes. The more compact the plot, the more your reader is on edge. So a writer must have an excellent editorial eye to fine-tune the loose ends and eliminate redundancies. This compact style is crucial to driving home the nail-biting sensation readers crave when they pick up your book. Hence creating an outline is necessary for an early diagnosis of what does not contribute to the page-turning tension of your narrative.

Here are some essential elements that new writers must take care of while outlining their thriller/horror fiction:

- **Create a compelling main character:** Despite the sounding cliche, a good thriller is riveted on the archetypal tension between the good guy and the bad guy. It can be the investigator versus the serial killer, the ghost with the unfinished business versus the guy who wronged it, or simply an innocent family versus an evil, malevolent haunted house. The stakes are high because the oppositional force is sometimes beyond human comprehension. The protagonist should be mentally strong and skilled enough to overcome the odds. To create an engaging character, devise a gripping backstory and chart their strengths and weaknesses. Remember, a thriller resides inside the head of the main character most of the time; hence make it a place your readers would enjoy living in.

- **Create an exciting antagonist:** A merely interesting protagonist is not enough; you have to pit them against an equal and opposite force – similar in attractiveness of the personality, opposite in motivations. Let the reader peel their character like peeling the layers of an onion instead of simply labeling them as the 'bad guy.' The central villain or antagonist should not be blandly evil but guided by their twisted logic and motivations, like Dr. Hannibal Lecter in *The Silence of the Lambs*. Through flashbacks, the reader learns that Hannibal Lecter's actions spring from severe trauma in the past, making him more than a psychopathic serial killer in the readers' eyes. If you can make the antagonist as understandable and motivated as your protagonist, you with have a crackling compound that will glue your readers' eyes to the page.

- **Hold the reader's attention in the opening scene:** An action-pact opening scene is crucial to reader engagement right from the beginning. Introduce the crime, the conflict/tension, and the stakes at the book's onset. Throw the reader in the middle of the action, then fill in the characters, character details, and other necessary information.

- **Build complications:** The writer of thrillers has a penchant for getting their protagonists in trouble. The central character must have some haunting memories, childhood trauma, heartbreak, or a severe psychological issue to deal with throughout the narrative. Remember, the higher the stakes the greater the reader's interest and the narrative satisfaction of seeing the protagonist overcome each hurdle at the end.
- **Add abundant twists and turns:** A thriller/horror plotline is a rollercoaster ride of plot twists and turns, intrigues and ulterior motives, turning points, and cliffhangers. These ups and downs may sound convoluted, but the idea is to understand the reader's expectations and thirst and take every care to quench them drop by drop because that keeps them turning the pages. Expecting the least expected is what makes a thriller/horror plot work.

H.P. LOVECRAFT AND HIS HANDWRITTEN HORROR

Different writers have different strategies for outlining. A fascinating and unique approach is shown in the outlining process of H.P. Lovecraft. The author of *The Call of Cthulhu, At the Mountains of Madness,* and others, was inspired by the work of Edgar Allen Poe, the master of creating horror and mystery in his poems and short stories. Lovecraft's outline looks as scary as his books but leads to immense success. One example page shows the text, with parts crossed out and key ideas circled like "GROUPS OF DOTS IN SNOW."

On the right, there are sketches with labels and even specific dimensions. His scribblings, drawings, strikethroughs, and seemingly haphazard-looking patterns of text and sketches make for a design or a blueprint more than a book outline. It looks graphic to some, cryptic to others, but makes perfect sense to Lovecraft's artistic sensibilities. An outline design only has to make sense to the writer.

THE STORY OF DEAN KOONTZ

If you are a horror/thriller enthusiast, it is improbable you do not have a couple of Dean Koontz books in your library. Koontz has written over 100 horror/thriller/suspense novels, 16 making it to the New Year Bestsellers List. An author who has tasted unprecedented success in this genre and is not a pantser but works on an elaborate book outlining principles. His *How to Write Bestselling Fiction* offers aspiring thriller/horror writers a four-step outlining formula. Let's take a closer look at Koontz's outlining guide:

- **Throw the main character into trouble as soon as possible:** Now, the type of trouble depends on your subgenre of choice, but it should be the worst possible predicament that your character can get in. It should affect the character's life most. For the caveat or the challenge to look grave to the reader, they must first have insight into the character's life, mind, and personality. So ensure your reader knows the character well enough to be affected by their predicament. Then the stakes will be high, and the reader will be on edge.
- **A simple solution is always dull.** Create a web of problems cascading logically from one seemingly agreeable solution. However, please don't force the difficulties; let them build up as a butterfly effect of the character's actions. Whatever they do to get out of trouble makes it worse: The momentum of problems should go up, not down; make sure your character's life gets worse, more complex with every attempt to make it easier.
- **The situation appears hopeless:** Make your character's life so complicated that even you, as the writer, have to wonder how to put an end to their misery. How to write them out of the predicament is the question that will keep your reader turning to the next page.
- **The hero succeeds or fails against all odds.** You must gratify the reader with a payoff from the setup

that precedes. Now, this part swings both ways – either the hero wins or fails, retaining their heroic dignity. For instance, a novel is about a captain and his sinking ship; he either saves the crew or sinks with the vessel. Either way, the reader is gratified as the protagonist either realizes from their tryst with the obstacles that things only seemed beyond repair or makes a heroic effort to fix what was really beyond repair.

This four-part formula can help new writers chart the course of their thriller/horror before they embark on the writing journey.

WORDS OF A BESTSELLER TEACHER

David Baldacci takes a fascinating approach to outlining a book. He confesses being in the middle of being the plotter and the pantser. Baldacci won't outline from A to Z, and he doesn't have the ending before he starts writing. He has two rudimentary binders – one for the broad strokes and the other for chapter-by-chapter detail. The first one has a panoramic view, a wider sweep of what he wants to achieve from the book. It's like setting some rough milestones in your journey without thinking of how to reach them all, or, like creating a rough sketch, you are yet to figure out the details of color and styling. The second binder carries all the nitty-gritty details that act as connectors or lubricants, making the more significant parts work together. The writer fills these in gradually after having the broader structure ready.

Baldacci also maintains that the best part of being a writer is the creative liberty you can take with your organizing principle. So being a pantser or a plotter or resting somewhere in between is ultimately an artistic decision particular to the writer in question.

Whatever the structuring logic or organizing principle you adopt, thriller and horror writers mustn't lose sight of their final objective – to create suspense, dread, and fear of a future crime or disaster. Remember, the reader is not looking for comfort or security through the narrative. Instead, they are looking for the opposite; they have signed up for a nail-biting experience and will only be satisfied to see the least expected.

10

OUTLINE ADVICE FOR WAR AND HISTORY NOVELS

A curious commingling of fact and fiction, historical accuracy, and artistic sensibility of the recorded past and its contemporary and highly subjective interrogation, historical fiction is the playing field of humanities and liberal arts disciplines. Historical fiction gives readers the chance to learn about history from the writer's viewpoint. Writers form their interpretation of history in fiction. There's always a debate between historical accuracy and historical adaptation. It will often spark curiosity and encourage readers to do their research into actual historical events, learn where fact gives way to fiction, and form their responses to and interpretation of history. Historical fiction is a highly provocative genre that requires immense historical awareness and intellectual curiosity by the writer because fictionalizing history is a great power that comes with even greater responsibility. Well, it's easier to get things wrong if you don't research.

HOW TO PREPARE YOUR HISTORICAL FICTION

Since you are dealing with events that have happened in the past and are archived and even preserved in communal memory, writing historical fiction can be like walking on thin ice. You can neither tamper with the history nor report it as it is. So, where do we draw the line? How to determine where fact ends and fiction begins? There are some ground rules which must be observed while planning your historical fiction. During the outlining phase, it's better to be aware of these do's and don'ts to avoid straying too far when the actual writing begins.

The first rule to remember is don't force history into the plot; make it contextual. It has to make sense to the world your novel needs to be set into. Before choosing an era for your human story to unfold, the timeline and setting must be thought through. This brings us to another important point – the writers of historical fiction need to gain some perspective on the fact that they are expected to focus on telling a human story, not recounting the events of history. Weave history into the very fabric of your account. How incidents unfold, and how your characters act or are acted upon.

An appropriate example would be Dickens's *A Tale of Two Cities*. Never for a moment does Dickens seem to read out of the pages of history. Yet the characters' destinies in the novel result from the social conditions propelling the French revolution and its aftermath. The smug indifference of aristocracy and the cold-blooded vengeance of the working class during the reign of terror are perfectly blended into Dickens's characterization and plot development.

The second and most important rule is to know what to exclude. There are boundaries between history and fiction that need to be respected. It would be best if you did not go overboard with either. For instance, if there's a historical event that looks somewhat unreasonable to the contemporary reader and which does not contribute any artistic or causal value to your work, it must be excluded for good. However, if such a facet must be retained, create a character who will voice the reader's disbelief or unwillingness to accept that part of history. While creating your character outline, it is essential to make some avant garde or rebel characters who do not fit into the epoch they were born in for all the right reasons. If every character is a product of their times, you are only promoting conformists and ignoring a crucial part of history – the nonconformists, the agents of change. However, if you create a rebel, give them the right causes to rebel.

Just as you must not go overboard with historicizing your story, you must also need to know the boundaries of fiction. Some events in history cannot be tampered with, no matter how essential it might seem to the fictional fabric of your work. Here comes the significance of thorough research. No matter the genre, research is integral to writing, but it is all the more crucial for historical fiction because the stakes are too high when you adapt what has already happened to create your fictional world. Impeccable research enables you to achieve historical accuracy. Historical accuracy is reflected in your descriptions of cutlery, architecture, attire, fashion, customs, social and economic life, politics, rituals, high art, and popular culture. So while outlining, keep extensive notes of the research database corresponding to each section/chapter.

First, you must decide on your approach to fictionalizing history; then, you can take a call on the extent. The limits of accuracy need to be set by the writers themselves because there are as many answers to 'how accurate a historical fiction should be as there are historical novels. And this decision is best taken during the outlining phase. Here are a few common approaches to historical fiction:

- A fictionalized but accurate version of history, as found in biographical historical fiction.
- Telling a fictional story with history as the backdrop; only the setting is real. The story's focus is on the fictional characters rather than any made-up renderings of the lives of real people from the past.
- You are using history to inspire your story rather than making it the story itself. You can base a character on a real person or an incident from the

past but make sure not to choose a real person or their life if they are still alive.
- Retelling a true story with some creative liberties is the most challenging; you can fabricate or twist essential elements of history, but you can always use your creativity to draw on the gaps in recorded history, subtext, and rumors.

There is a difference between filling the gaps and distorting facts. The writer should trace those gaps during their research and try to build the narrative around the mysteries of history. History is open to interpretation if you can substantiate your understanding of it. However, the bounds of plausibility must be adhered to. As per historical records, you cannot make a character show up at an incident years before they arrived unless you are prepared for some historical backlash. Then again, Quentin Tarantino did some major historical juggling with his movie Inglorious Basterds, which was critically acclaimed.

A significant point to remember while writing historical fiction is respecting reader interest in terms of language use. The irony is that you cannot stick to historical accuracy in choosing the communication medium for your characters. If your novel is set in the 14th century and you make them speak in Chaucerian English, your reader engagement will be in jeopardy.

Similarly, when your 14th-century characters talk in the English that your colleagues, neighbors or friends speak, the reader will be equally appalled by the historical inaccuracies. Choose a language that is understandable but not from a certain period and not modern slang. Well, the answer lies here in a bit of linguistic jugglery. You must avoid modern colloquialisms and look for a tone and vocabulary that feels at home in your epoch of choice and the contemporary era. Use archaisms just as much as needed to convey a feeling of that period and blend it into the modern reader's language of choice.

WILLIAM FAULKNER'S *A FABLE* OUTLINE

Outlining is not always a studied and methodical process; it can be highly spontaneous and slightly eccentric. Faulkner presented a brilliant example of such creativity when he created an outline for his book *A Fable* on the walls of his study. Yes, first-hand scribblings on the walls went into the outline for his Pulitzer prize-winning book. Each section was titled with a day of the week, and sentences and short texts were under each day. He started the work on this novel set in France during the First World War, just after the end of the Second World War. The story kept him occupied for a decade. The scribblings on the wall helped him get immersed in the plotting and chronology of the novel. However, his wife was not so happy and painted over the walls. So

Faulkner rewrote the entire outline and shellacked the wall to preserve the records.

EDITING A CHILDREN'S WAR STORY

Few people know that the author of the famous *War Horse* wrote children's books. He wanted to write a story from the horse's viewpoint that captured the friendships between horse and owner and the stories of World War I veterans. War is always a controversial, sensitive, and complex subject. The challenges redouble, especially if the target readers are relatively young.

So making the storyline suitable for a young audience was the biggest stumbling block for writer Michael Morpurgo. The handwritten outline shows words and whole sentences crossed out and rewritten, showing that nothing is set in stone, not even an overview. The revisions and re-revisions are primarily directed toward finding the right tone for the book.

Hence, as a new writer, if you believe outlining can limit the creative possibilities, it's time to rethink the position. Outlining is more about putting your thoughts on paper so you can give them a second, third, or as many reviews as you wish to.

THE PILLARS OF KEN FOLLETT'S OUTLINES

Let's look at another planner to further illustrate the value of planning. British writer Ken Follet loves to call himself a great planner for all the right reasons. Before writing a single word of a book, he devotes an entire year to research. The research gives him ideas on plot lines, characters, and scenes. For Follett, researching and planning go hand in hand because while working on the book plan, he might realize he does not know enough about a particular topic. So he will read up some more before proceeding. He also prefers visiting real locations while outlining his historical novels. While researching his novel *Evening and Morning*, he spent a week touring the Anglo-Saxon buildings in England and took a trip to the Viking Ship Museum in Norway.

At the end of such an eventful year of reading field trips and planning, his outline will be around 60 pages, containing the main characters and what happens to them in each chapter. Elaborate, extensive, and meticulous, this kind of initial investment in planning and research is bound to pay off any writer at a more advanced stage of writing their books.

Lastly, while outlining a historical novel, the timeline can be the trickiest part to handle. A visual timeline can be helpful, especially with moveable elements, like flashcards or drag and-drop software. Using these tools that allow you to rethink and reorganize, you can create a foolproof timeline for your historical novel.

11

OUTLINE ADVICE FOR CRIME AND DETECTIVE NOVELS

In terms of effects or the impact on the reader, crime and detective fiction have the same agenda as horror and thrillers – to leave the reader on the edge of their seats, turning the pages desperately to know what happens next. The goal is to ensure maximum reader engagement. Hence from outlining to editing the first draft, filtering out redundancies and those parts that make the tempo of the narrative drop. A compact outline enables you to create an intimate reading experience for your audience. So outlining is crucial to writing a suspense or crime novel. So let's deep dive into the most efficient outlining process for your writing.

TEMPLATES FOR YOUR CRIME NOVELS

By now, you know the significance of the three-act structure and how integral it is to plot development and to create an organizing principle or outline for your book. Let me make your job easier with a more streamlined approach to building your book outline. First, create a workable template for arranging your content by defining what goes into which part of the three-act structure.

Act I:

- Present the crime
- Introduce the detective
- Provide plausible options for suspects
- Bring in some complications around the crime
- Introduce a private life subplot or a backstory

Act II:

- Early investigation and interrogation providing initial leads or cues
- The suspect disappears
- The plot thickens: complication becomes more serious, raising the stakes
- The subplot thickens/develops

Act III:

- Hidden motives of all involved come to the fore
- Unsatisfactory solutions are reached
- Return to an overlooked clue
- Subplot resolved
- Confrontation with the criminal/antagonist/perpetrator
- Denouement/resolution

I already discussed the several online tools and software available for organizing the book outline. Writing a novel and keeping track of all the characters and every angle of the plot development is a colossal task and outlining makes this job more manageable. There is a large variety of free templates available online that can be useful to the new writer for creating mystery/crime novel outlines. Crime outlining templates are available for free on the internet and they look somewhat like this:

1. Set up (backstory)

1. The main character has a single goal to accomplish
2. The murderer has a motive to kill the victim
3. The victim affected many characters' lives (suspects 1, 2, and 3 with plausible motives)
4. Supporting characters
5. Subplot

2. A murder/crime is committed

1. How?
2. Why?
3. Where?
4. How did the murderer/criminal cover it up?

3. Main characters are brought together

1. Location/setting
2. What brings them together?
3. How is the victim's body discovered/crime revealed?
4. What is the murderer/criminal doing?
5. The main character's goal can be achieved by solving the mystery/murder

4. Suspects are revealed

1. Suspect 1 had some old score to settle with the victim
2. Suspect 2 had an ulterior motive of gaining something from the victim's murder
3. Suspect 3 reveals a deception
4. An overlooked clue points to the murder
5. How does the subplot evolve?

Using these organized templates allows you to be meticulous without worrying about which details you left out. The template covers all the plot points, tropes, and story elements in the proper causal sequence of unfolding. Once you organize your material as per the template, you get to visualize the whole story in a nutshell. You may think that all stories would become boring and predictable if done like this, but it's tried and tested and works well.

MORE THAN AN INSPIRATION FOR NOVEL OUTLINING

Agatha Christie taught herself to read and write despite her mother's wishes. Though a highly imaginative kid living in her world of imaginary friends, she had no ambition to become a writer. She wrote about the world she knew, finding inspiration from "odd moments." Her first work was published when she was 11, a poem she wrote in bed sick with the flu.

Christie claims that an idea can hit you at the oddest of places. Anything and everything she observed in her world could turn into a potential idea for a book. So how did these ideas transform into full-length books? The answer is endless note-taking. She kept dozens of notebooks where she would write down ideas about plots and characters when they came to her. She had over a hundred notebooks all over, out of which 73 have survived. These notebooks offer a peek into the mindscape of Christie, her creative process, and a wealth of unpublished materials.

This great writer of detective and mystery novels spent more time planning her books than writing them. Her notebooks stand witness to the planning and thought that went into her writing process. She will always be in her mindscape, thinking plotlines, details, clues, and at best, jotting them down in those notebooks. Her son-in-law Anthony Hicks once said that, unlike other writers, she would never shut herself away, "You never saw her write."

For writing a mystery novel, be ready to have ideas and clues all the time. Always keep your writing material handy and jot down any idea you get in the raw – you never know when the muse finds you!

HOW AN ARCTIC TRIP WAS THE MUSE BEHIND SHERLOCK HOLMES

Some experiences become formative influences on you from which you emerge as an artist, and the whaling expedition did just that for Doyle. For writing or any creative art, you never know where inspiration can strike you, and the same happened with Arthur Conan Doyle when he went on an Arctic whaling voyage in 1880. He was a medical student, and every whaling ship had to have a surgeon on board. His friend couldn't go and offered Conan Doyle the job. During his time on the boat, the young medical student experienced sights and sounds, events and incidents that stayed with him forever in his eternal creation – the Sherlock Holmes books. Throughout the voyage, he maintained a journal which, after his descendants agreed to reveal it to the world, opened up a new window into the life and mind of our favorite writer of detective fiction. His vivid diary with grim details and drawings later became the Sherlock Holmes books still loved today. The journal is full of Doyle's experiences and gory details of the day-to-day activities on the whaler. There are shocking descriptions of scenes of seals, polar bears, narwhals, and medium-sized whales being killed with abandon. There were days when Doyle would come covered in animal blood frozen on his skin and clothes and could only be washed off after thawing. After these experiences cultivated Sherlock Holmes, Doyle admitted in a letter to his mother that now he could live anywhere in the world and eat anything.

As a writer, you must be open to the external world and how it reaches you. The transfusion of the outside experience into your creative fabric can give you your masterpiece. Like many other writers, Doyle has benefitted from journaling his days, the best way to preserve your lived experiences.

THE QUEEN OF IRISH CRIME FICTION

The creative process varies from writer to writer, but most of the time, it's a self-chosen lonely path. America-Irish writer Tana French whose first book was released in 2007, approaches the creative process in this manner. Though ideally not a big fan of structuring outlining, French retains a general form or shape, atmosphere, pace, and mood of the story. She admittedly starts her book with a few vague ideas in place and lets them take on a shape as she moves farther into the narrative. At this stage, she prefers not to share her story ideas with anyone (except her husband). She believes an editor can add value to a finished work only after the writer has given it life on paper. So intermediate rounds of discussion and review can hardly benefit the writing process. Since there's no coherent design or structure, it's better to keep the ideation part to yourself and approach the reader/editor only with a finished draft.

This approach to writing is closer to the pantser style, yet the significance of having complete clarity on the general look and feel of the book cannot be ignored. This writing style gives you a lot of creative liberties and emphasizes the power of revision and editing in adding value to your manuscript. The editor does not make a new work out of your book; they help the writer reach what they desire. And until the writer writes it down, it's hard for the editor to know what that desire is.

With book outlining, there is no one right or wrong formula; I cannot emphasize this enough. But there are some genre-specific pros and cons involved in these standard approaches to outlining. For instance, the risk with not having an outline for the suspense/crime/detective genre is that you keep adding plots, subplots, and twists without an end in sight. While the result might make sense to the writer, the reader could feel this is too much. You can overwhelm the reader with too much to process in too little time. In your bid to create an engaging reading experience, you may do the exact opposite, exhausting the reader. Also, not having an outline risks spoiling the rationale behind the resolution. Your investigator gets to the criminal by following clues and using their intellect. That process should be conceived flawlessly without making it appear too easy for the detective. Hence, the writer should know who did it from the beginning and take good care that the reader doesn't know until the moment of clarity.

12

OUTLINE ADVICE FOR POPULAR FICTION

Popular fiction has no one style or voice or general tenor. It does have one golden rule, though – it has to appeal to the audience. As it is, that's the broadest, vaguest, and most open-ended objective you can have in mind before starting a book. But to write popular fiction, you must know the ropes of creating a book that appeals to the mass market. This appeal requires a particular type of planning as you are about to address a wide range of readers. Popular fiction is equally broad; it can be a range of different genres, and sometimes, even a mix of different genres in one book. The audience of popular fiction is looking for plots full of complications and conflicts, elements of surprise and a wish-fulfillment or shocking ending, and all of it dished out in an easy-read yet aesthetic language. Planning a book in this genre is essential as to cater to such a diverse audience with so many expectations, you must follow some general guidelines for outlining.

Before getting into that general rulebook, let's look closely at what makes a novel appealing to the mass market.

WHAT MAKES A NOVEL THAT APPEALS TO THE MANY

Looking at J. K. Rowling, the highest-paid author in the world whose net worth is just a slither short of a billion dollars, it might seem that writing is a moneymaking business, and all the famous writers are wealthy. This notion is partially true; if your book becomes a bestseller, you can make a fortune for yourself. However, the chances of becoming a wealthy published author are rare, so you need to know the odds you are playing against.

Creating a bestseller is a challenge; you need to find answers to what is mass readership? What can make so many people worldwide want to read a particular book at one point in time? How are the authors writing such commercial success? It won't be an overstatement to say that everyone is looking for the next bestseller in the publishing world. So what constitutes one? Despite the genre, there is a specific pattern behind a book becoming a bestseller, which a computer algorithm can detect.

Commissioning editor and Stanford scholar Jodie Archer has been in the book business for a long time and came up with this finding. With book mining expert Matthew Jockers, she has written a near-accurate algorithm that can tell whether or not a manuscript will hit the NY Times bestsellers list. The algorithm answered with 90% certainty for authors like J. K. Rowling or *Fifty Shades* fame EL James that their works will be bestsellers. To identify what the bestselling authors had in common, the algorithm analyzed 280,000 data points of popular books. And the results point toward the recipe of a bestseller. The writers must consciously use shorter sentences, voice-driven narratives, and less erudite vocabulary than literary fiction. Bestsellers have an emotional beat! If you can devise a symmetrical pattern of emotional highs and lows in your book, your readers will be hooked to it. The algorithm also identifies a limited gallery of topics that recur in different combinations in a bestseller, and most successful authors stick to one topic. One of the most popular topics is human closeness, as exemplified by the success of Milly Johnson's works. Human relationships are at the core of bestsellers; if your audience cannot relate to the emotional journeys your characters undertake, they feel emotionally flat at the end. That's why I would say friendship and love are as integral a part of the *Harry Potter* novels (and, of course, the movie series adapted from the books) as is magic!

WHAT DOES A POPULAR FICTION NOVEL NEED?

The secret to writing a bestseller is to hit the sweet spot on character, style, plot, and theme. Easier said than done, and this takes a thorough understanding of how the different story elements of a popular fiction book work together. A popular fiction story's five key story elements include character, situation, objective, opponent, and disaster. These five elements are ubiquitous in all kinds of popular fiction. So let us try to identify each component of a book we remember dearly – *The Lion King*.

- **Character:** Simba, the young cub of the King Mufasa
- **Situation:** The plains of Africa
- **Objective:** To become the King
- **Opponent:** Scar, the evil uncle
- **Disaster:** Scar took control of the Plains and driven it to spoils

The character is the protagonist whose journey is lived by the reader. Hence character outlining plays a crucial role in popular fiction. If you do not give your character an emotional depth, matching moral strength, intellectual capacity, and vulnerability, the readers will not be invested in their journey. In the instance, the reader emotionally connects with Simba and follows him from being a wee cub to a mighty King, and roots for him all along. The reader feels his pain at losing his father and how the young cub is manipulated into believing it was his fault. Simba's guilt makes him vulnerable and more relatable. His objective is to regain what his father stood for and what's rightfully his – becoming the King. The disaster he faces is his usurping evil uncle Scar, who orchestrates the death of Simba's father, Mufasa, and makes the cub believe it was his fault, driving him away from the jungle. So how can the readers empathize with Simba if the writer doesn't write Scar as the vilest and most vicious character? Defeating Scar and getting back what's due becomes as much the reader's objective as Simba's. All this human drama in the lives of our animal characters unfolds in the aptest setting, the plains of Africa, not just Africa but Pride Rock. The setting is carefully contrived to bring the whole story to life.

While outlining, the popular fiction writer must be cognizant of these five elements. Create a template with each item and keep jotting down details under each component. The details will grow as you go ahead with your research.

JODI PICOULT AND HER STRUCTURE

Jodi Picoult is one writer of popular fiction who isn't scared to try new methods to capture a wider audience. She has a penchant for treating novel or even controversial subject matters. She mainly uses negative issues and turns them around into problems relevant to the contemporary world. When she wrote *My Sisters Keepers*, the concept of designer babies was alien to the world in 2004 (and it still is). Picoult has several writing techniques that startle the reader. One technique was a chapter with just one word. It won't make sense unless you read the book, but it works.

She creates bestsellers from the most unconventional ideas with her exceptional writing talent and analytical insight into apparently controversial opinions. Picoult is famous because she writes intriguing yet believable stories about complex and contemporary issues. What's more, she takes the controversy and makes it logical. These subjects are often taboo subjects that people are uncomfortable discussing, but her characters are relatable, making it possible.

As for her writing process, Picoult makes no secret that she sets out with an ending in her mind, but often she is wrong! This means beginning with a particular destination in mind does not curb your creative energies; you can always arrive at a different ending altogether if it works for your book. Picoult is a writer who dwells somewhere between the planner and pantser zones. She begins with a probing what-if question and keeps pushing it until she has solid leads to a good story. She doesn't start the writing process until she has an excellent opening line. Then she keeps going chapter-by-chapter, developing each scene and plot line as needed. This writing practice is highly research reliant, and Picoult leaves no stone unturned for hers. The answers to the what-if questions direct her research via the internet, emails, and even visiting the exact places her book needs her to go (even death row in a prison). Another interesting observation made by Picoult is that the book takes on its own life after a certain time, as though it's writing itself. About two-thirds down the complete word count, the characters take over and lead the narrative, and it's better not to fight them because they do a better job living their own story!

Writers like Picoult reside in a very curious zone of creativity. Don't be misled into thinking that such writers do not have a plan and go with the flow. The answers to the what-if questions, extensive research, and building from the first sentence into a chaptered book like the snowflake technique are evidence of a plan, but a different one from having a 60-page outline.

So even if it's a William Shakespeare play or a Dan Brown, Danielle Steel, or Enid Blyton book, the secret to becoming a literary classic or a popular commercial success lies in an intricate design and pattern. A detailed outline unlocks creativity and allows the writer to explore every element in depth and select the path that best works for the book.

OUTLINE CONCLUSION

If you have been with me so far, you know what a book outline can do for your writing process. It's like thinking aloud on a piece of paper, a Word doc, or a readymade or customized outlining tool or template available online. The idea is to get your thoughts in one place to streamline the creative process, and any media of your choice works as long as it works for you. Different writers have different ways of visualizing their story outlines, and each works for the individual writer, given their creative temperament. So I introduced you to a broad bandwidth of writers, from plotters to pantsers, representing two creative extremes. Plotters are ardent and meticulous planners who need to visualize the end before the beginning and all the intermediate steps which take them to the end. The pantsers have to have a moment of clarity or an idea, one which the entire book develops. The writing takes on its own life as they proceed. However, several intermediate styles can combine both schools of thought in different ratios. We learned about the different writers – gardeners, architects, designers, and weavers. The gardeners believe in the organic growth of a book, while architects have to have a thorough plan. The designers stand somewhere in-between. They have a rough idea or sketch, not the complete picture; eventually, the details are filled in. The knitters are always trying out different design combinations and doing patchwork wherever needed.

Writing is a highly subjective method, and hence there can be as many outlining techniques as there are writers. Despite that, we attempted to list some major outlining strategies to benefit new writers. You can take some elements or the entire method from each while outlining your book. It can also be a combination of two ways. So we discussed a dozen outlining strategies like snowflake, agenda, bookend, tree, and the three acts method. Each method has its way of channelizing and organizing the writer's thought process. Whatever your fiction genre or whatever outlining principle you follow, fiction books always have a broad three-act structure. We also discussed the online tools and software for devising timelines for your books. One fascinating approach to outlining is to give it a physical, visual form using flashcards, spreadsheets, and drag-and-drop software to keep your outlines handy for revision.

Just as outlining methods vary with writers, they also vary with genres. Hence we discussed a wide range of outlining basics specific to different fiction genres. For example, we saw how historical novels are be outlined by maintaining a perfect balance between the historical context and the fictional content. If based on real-life personalities, the timelining details or the characters cannot be tampered with. Components cannot be fictionalized to the extent of implausibility.

Similarly, for horror, mystery, thriller, crime, and detective novels, I suggested some ready-to use templates to organize the story from incident to revelation, keeping the plot's momentum thickening until the final disclosure. But a romance novel must follow a different trajectory of beginning with a meet-cute, proceeding through false hope and disappointment until the characters come together. For popular fiction, the oscillations of the emotional high and lows of the characters and the human relationships are integral plot elements that must be paid attention to while designing the outline.

The extensive discussion reveals that all the varied fiction genres have a few elements in common which must be included in the outlining template: protagonist, setting, goals, complications, timeline, antagonist, subplot, interrelationships between major and minor characters, and resolution. Keeping all these elements in your outlining template and adding to each as you proceed with your research seems like an excellent way. We also learned about the outlining techniques of different celebrity and bestselling authors. While Jo Rowling is an ardent plotter, Stephen King is a pantser. Jodi Picoult's approach lies somewhere between, and she follows the snowflake method in her writing. While *Sherlock Holmes* is the outcome of Doyle's experiences and journaling on the whaling expedition, William Faulkner used his office walls to jot down outlines. Each eccentric genius to his own!

The purpose of acquainting you with all these diverse techniques is to understand that there's no right or wrong way to organize your material; you have to identify which method works for you. Suppose it doesn't seem to work; investing a reasonable amount of time in outlining speeds up the writing process and improves the quality of your work. Whatever the process, it does not interfere with creativity; instead, outlines allow you the flexibility to rethink and be open to changing any character track or plot element.

If it looks like a lot of work, remember that there's no need to have a fancy outlining document. It can be a bulleted list, an excel spreadsheet, many sticky notes on a display board, and a mind map you can read and figure. Remember, the outline is not up for publishing; the book is. So devise your working method as per your convenience. You have to start with a scratch, the first key sentence, and the rest will fall in place.

The reading community is looking for different kinds of books, and writing is an evolving art that must grow better with every published one. So, aspiring fellow writers who carried some wisdom from this book are requested to return some in their turn. There is nothing better for me than someone reading and benefitting from my work, but publishing books is a one-sided form of communication. Please let me know if you have gained anything from this book with a review. I can't learn unless I receive your feedback. Share your ideas, your thoughts, and what more could be included in the outlining techniques in your reviews. Who knows your reviews could open up discussions for the emergence of new ideas that will help up-and coming writers kick start their careers. Let's keep the ball rolling!

FREE GIFT

How to clearly organize your story ideas into an epic book you can write and publish
By John S. Warner

Just for You!
A FREE GIFT TO OUR READERS

Please enjoy this 20-page workbook to create the best positive Character arc for your protagonist. Easy to follow Step by Step Guide

Scan the QR code below

Or go to https://johnswarner.activehosted.com/f/1.

MORE FROM JOHN S WARNER

The Secrets to Creating Character Arcs

The Secrets to Outlining your Novel

The Secrets to Creating Character Arcs Workbook

Available on Amazon.com

BIBLIOGRAPHY

12-great-ways-to-outline-a-novel/. (n.d.). https://Thejohnfox.Com. https://thejohnfox.com/2020/01/12-great ways-to-outline-a-novel/

12-ways-to-end-a-chapter. (n.d.). https://Thejohnfox.Com. https://thejohnfox.com/2018/07/12-ways-to-end-a chapter/

Ackerman, A. (2014, May 27). *michael-crichtons-method-plotting-story*. Https://Writershelpingwriters.Net. https://writershelpingwriters.net/2014/05/michael-crichtons-method-plotting-story/

Ackerman, A. (2017, April 6). *The Efficient Writer: Using Timelines to Organize Story Details*. Https://Writershelpingwriters.Net/2017/04/the-Efficient-Writer-Using-Timelines-to-Organize-Story Details/. https://writershelpingwriters.net/2017/04/the-efficient-writer-using-timelines-to-organize story-details/

Baldacci, D. (n.d.). *Outlining*. Https://Www.Masterclass.Com. https://www.masterclass.com/classes/david baldacci-teaches-mystery-and-thriller-writing/chapters/outlining#

Bannan, S. (2015, June 11). *Tana French: 'I love the Eureka! moment when I realise that what she's suggesting is perfect.'* Https://Www.Irishtimes.Com. https://www.irishtimes.com/culture/books/tana-french-i-love the-eureka-moment-when-i-realise-that-what-she-s-suggesting-is-perfect-1.2246322

Brown, D. (2021a, September 8). *How to Outline your Novel*. Https://Www.Masterclass.Com. https://www.masterclass.com/articles/how-to-outline-your-novel#what-is-a-novel-outline

Brown, D. (2021b, September 13). *How to Choose a Plot Outline Method: 4 Techniques for Outlining Novels*. Https://Www.Masterclass.Com. https://www.masterclass.com/articles/4-techniques-for-outlining novels#4-classic-methods-of-creating-a-novel-outline

Brown, D. (2021c, September 13). *How to Choose a Plot Outline Method: 4 Techniques for Outlining Novels*. Https://Www.Masterclass.Com. https://www.masterclass.com/articles/4-techniques-for-outlining novels#4-classic-methods-of-creating-a-novel-outline

Chapter Length Matters. Here's Why. (2017, October 18). Https://Blog.Reedsy.Com. https://blog.reedsy.com/how-long-should-a-chapter-be/ *collection-items/war-horse-by-michael-morpurgo-first-manuscript-draft-and-typescript-draft*. (n.d.). Https://Www.Bl.Uk. https://www.bl.uk/collection-items/war-horse-by-michael-morpurgo-first manuscript-draft-and-typescript-draft

Cron, L. (2016, August 9). *Story Genius: How to Use Brain Science to Go Beyond Outlining and Write a Riveting Novel (Before You Waste Three Years Writing 327 Pages That Go Nowhere) Paperback – August 9, 2016.* Ten Speed Press.

Davenport, B. (2020, June 10). *165 Must-Use Character Development Questions For Writers.* Https://Authority.Pub. https://authority.pub/character-development-questions/

difference between outline and first draft. (2008, January 25). Https://Www.Reddit.Com. https://www.reddit.com/r/writing/comments/q1uduq/difference_between_outline_and_first_draft/ Donaldson, J. (n.d.). *your-questions-answered/*. Https://Www.Juliadonaldson.Co.Uk. https://www.juliadonaldson.co.uk/about-me/your-questions-answered/

Dr. Seuss Book: Yes, They Found It in a Box. (n.d.). Https://Www.Nytimes.Com. https://www.nytimes.com/2015/07/22/books/dr-seuss-book-a-discovery-in-a-box-and-then-a reconstruction.html

english/courses-children/resources/attention-span. (n.d.). Https://Www.Britishcouncil.My. https://www.britishcouncil.my/english/courses-children/resources/attention-span

Five Key Story Elements – Examples from Popular Fiction. (2016, July 28). Https://Www.Novel-Software.Com. https://www.novel-software.com/story-elements/

Fouke, J. (n.d.). *naming-chapters-pros-and-cons.* Https://Www.How-to-Write-a-Book-Now.Com/. https://www.how-to-write-a-book-now.com/naming-chapters-pros-and-cons.html

Furgerson, D. (2017, September 23). *Want to write a bestselling novel? Use an algorithm.* Https://Www.Theguardian.Com. https://www.theguardian.com/money/2017/sep/23/write-bestselling novel-algorithm-earning-money

Hamand, M. (2012, January 24). *Creative Writing For Dummies.* For Dummies.

Hoare, P. (2012, September 15). *Conan Doyle the seal clubber: Revealed in a grip-*

ping diary the blood-soaked voyage to the Arctic that inspired one of Sherlock Holmes' most chilling mysteries.

Https://Www.Dailymail.Co.Uk. https://www.dailymail.co.uk/news/article-2203597/Conan-Doyle-seal clubber-Revealed-gripping-diary-blood-soaked-voyage-Arctic-inspired-Sherlock-Holmes-chilling mysteries.html

How Christie Wrote. (n.d.). Https://Www.Agathachristie.Com. https://www.agathachristie.com/about christie/how-christie-wrote

How To Create A Plot Outline In 8 Easy Steps. (n.d.). Https://Www.How-to-Write-a-Book-Now.Com. https://www.how-to-write-a-book-now.com/plot-outline.html

How to Create a Vivid Setting for Your Story. (2021, August 3). Https://Www.Masterclass.Com. https://www.masterclass.com/articles/how-to-create-a-vivid-setting-for-your-story#how-to-create-a vivid-setting-for-your-story

How to Outline a Novel: an Author's Guide. (2022, March 10). Https://Blog.Reedsy.Com. https://blog.reedsy.com/how-to-outline-a-book/

How to Outline Your Novel with Save the Cat! (n.d.). Https://Www.Savannahgilbo.Com. https://www.savannahgilbo.com/blog/plotting-save-the-cat

How to Structure Chapters of Your Novel: 8 Tips for Writing Chapters. (2021, August 9). Https://Www.Masterclass.Com. https://www.masterclass.com/articles/how-to-structure-chapters-of your-novel#how-to-structure-the-chapters-of-your-novel

How to Write a Thriller: 5 Tips for Writing a Gripping Thriller. (2021, November 11). Https://Www.Masterclass.Com. https://www.masterclass.com/articles/how-to-write-a-thriller#8-types of-thrillers

How to Write the Plot for a Children's Book. (2021, August 9). Https://Www.Masterclass.Com. https://www.masterclass.com/articles/how-to-write-the-plot-for-a-childrens-book#how-to-write-the plot-for-a-childrens-book

how-to-outline-your-book-with-what-if-questions-use-these-4-step. (n.d.). Https://Thewritingkylie.Com. https://thewritingkylie.com/blog/how-to-outline-your-book-with-what-if-questions-use-these-4-step

how-to-write-a-mystery-novel-outline. (n.d.). Https://Www.Novel-Software.Com. https://www.novel software.com/how-to-write-a-mystery-novel-outline/

h-p-lovecrafts-monster-drawings. (2015, August 18). Https://Www.Openculture.Com. https://www.openculture.com/2015/08/h-p-lovecrafts-monster-drawings.html

jane-austens-novels-plot-construction. (2017, August 21). Https://Phdessay.Com. https://phdessay.com/jane austens-novels-plot-construction/

Jenkins, J. (n.d.). *character-development*. Https://Jerryjenkins.Com. https://jerryjenkins.com/character development/

Lai, J. (n.d.). *bookends-technique*. Https://Penandthepad.Com. https://penandthepad.com/bookends-technique 6140862.html

Lane, A. (2020, January 15). *5 planning tools for novel writing: Scrivener, Scapple, Xmind, Aeon Timeline and Trello*. Https://Medium.Com. https://medium.com/5by5/5-planning-tools-for-novel-writing-scrivener scapple-xmind-aeon-timeline-and-trello-ae566ce8af4

Layne, L. (2019, September). *Romance Novel Blueprint*. Https://Static.Showit.Co.

https://static.showit.co/file/Qk78LEGMRZO-qhnGCI9EzQ/62998/lauren_layne_-_template_-_romance_blueprint_-_september_2019.pdf

Noakes, A. (2020, July 14). *dos-and-donts-of-writing-historical-fiction*. Https://Www.Janefriedman.Com. https://www.janefriedman.com/dos-and-donts-of-writing-historical-fiction/

Noaks, A. (n.d.). *how-to-write-historical-fiction-in-10-steps/*. Https://Thehistoryquill.Com.

https://thehistoryquill.com/how-to-write-historical-fiction-in-10-steps/

novel-outline-template. (n.d.). Https://Www.Template.Net. https://www.template.net/business/outline templates/novel-outline-template/

Patterson, A. (2016, December 16). *How A Timeline Helps You Plot A Novel*. Https://Www.Writerswrite.Co.Za/How-a-Timeline-Helps-You-When-You-Plot/.

https://www.writerswrite.co.za/how-a-timeline-helps-you-when-you-plot/

Picoult, J. (n.d.). *FAQs*. Https://Www.Jodipicoult.Com. https://www.jodipicoult.com/faqs.html Reeder, E. (2022, June 11). *what-is-popular-fiction*. Https://Www.Languagehumanities.Org/. https://www.languagehumanities.org/what-is-popular-fiction.htm

Roald Dahl's Writing Style & Themes. (n.d.). Https://Roalddahlpresentation.Weebly.Com. https://roalddahlpresentation.weebly.com/style-themes.html

BIBLIOGRAPHY | 175

Russell, G. (2022, June 10). *Outline a Children's Book – 5 Story Mapping Success Tips*. Https://Self Publishingschool.Com. https://self-publishingschool.com/outline-a-childrens-book/

S. (2021, February 13). *testing-dean-koontzs-story-structure*. Http://Scottwritesstuff.Com. http://scottwritesstuff.com/2021/02/13/testing-dean-koontzs-story-structure/

Setting_(narrative). (n.d.). Https://En.Wikipedia.Org. https://en.wikipedia.org/wiki/Setting_(narrative) Smailes, G. (n.d.). *snowflake-method*. Https://Bubblecow.Com. https://bubblecow.com/blog/snowflake-method Small, J. (2020, September 22). *Ken Follett's Secret Formula for Writing Success*. Https://Www.Entrepreneur.Com. https://www.entrepreneur.com/article/356563

Sparks, N. (n.d.). *Learn the Craft*. Https://Nicholassparks.Com/for-Writers/Learn-the-Craft/. https://nicholassparks.com/for-writers/learn-the-craft/

subgenres-of-horror-films-explained. (n.d.). Https://Www.Lafilm.Edu/Blog. https://www.lafilm.edu/blog/subgenres-of-horror-films-explained/

Three Act Structure: How to Nail This Story Structure in 3 Steps. (n.d.). Https://Www.Dailywritingtips.Com/Three-Act-Structure/. https://www.dailywritingtips.com/three-act structure/

Timeline. (n.d.). Https://En.Wikipedia.Org. https://en.wikipedia.org/wiki/Timeline

Victor, W. (2009). *Creative Writing Now Character Outline*. Https://Www.Creative-Writing-Now.Com. https://www.creative-writing-now.com/support-files/character_outline_from_creative_writing_now.pdf Weiland, K. M. (2011, July 1). *Outlining Your Novel: Map Your Way to Success (Helping Writers Become Authors) Paperback – July 1, 2011*. PenForASword.

Weiland, K. M. (2016, October 24). *How to Find and Fill All Your Plot Holes (How to Outline for NaNoWriMo, Pt. 4)*. Https://Www.Helpingwritersbecomeauthors.Com/.

https://www.helpingwritersbecomeauthors.com/nanowrimo-guide-outlining-plot-holes/ *what should be included in a main character outline?* (n.d.). Https://Www.How-to-Write-a-Book Now.Com/What-Should-Be-Included-in-a-Main-Character-Outline.Html. https://www.how-to-write-a book-now.com/what-should-be-included-in-a-main-character-outline.html

What-makes-Jodi-Picoult-such-a-successful-writer. (n.d.). Https://Www.Quora.Com. https://www.quora.com/What-makes-Jodi-Picoult-such-a-successful-writer

william-faulkner-outlines-on-his-office-wall-the-plot-of-a-fable. (2015, February 12). Https://Www.Openculture.Com. https://www.openculture.com/2015/02/william-faulkner-outlines-on his-office-wall-the-plot-of-a-fable.html

Yang, H. (2021, September 25). *How to Create a Romance Novel Outline*. Https://Prowritingaid.Com. https://prowritingaid.com/romance-novel-outline

Printed in Great Britain
by Amazon